Game of My Life
VIRGINIA TECH

Mike Harris

Foreword by Frank Beamer

SportsPublishingLLC.com

ISBN-10: 1-59670-004-1
ISBN-13: 978-1-59670-004-8

All interior photos are courtesy of Virginia Tech Sports Information

Publishers: Peter L. Bannon and Joseph J. Bannon Sr.
Senior managing editor: Susan M. Moyer
Acquisitions editor: John Humenik
Developmental editor: Doug Hoepker
Art director: K. Jeffrey Higgerson
Dust jacket design: Heidi Norsen
Interior layout: Kathryn R. Holleman
Photo editor: Erin Linden-Levy

Printed in the United States of America

Sports Publishing L.L.C.
804 North Neil Street
Champaign, IL 61820
Phone: 1-877-424-2665
Fax: 217-363-2073
SportsPublishingLLC.com

Library of Congress Cataloging-in-Publication Data

Harris, Mike, 1956-
    Game of my life, Virginia Tech / Mike Harris.
      p. cm.
    ISBN 1-59670-004-1 (hardcover : alk. paper)
    1. Virginia Tech Hokies (Football team) 2. Football players--United States--Biography. I. Title.
  GV958.V54H37 206
  796.332'6309755'785--dc22
                    2006019325

To Sue, David, and Courtney—
They know all about me and love me just the same

CONTENTS

BASKETBALL

FOREWORD

I graduated from and played football at Virginia Tech. I'm preparing for my 20th season as head football coach here. I raised my family here. I love this school and it has been a huge part of my life. I love to talk about Virginia Tech and I enjoy reading about Virginia Tech.

Many of the athletes featured in *Game of My Life: Virginia Tech* played for me. A couple played with me, and one of them *is* me. Even though I know their stories, I had fun reading about them and the important games they experienced in a Tech uniform. I learned a few things along the way, too. It was a real pleasure reading about the athletes who preceded me here as well. Virginia Tech has a rich history, as evidenced by the likes of Dickie Beard, Carroll Dale, Chris Smith, Glen Combs, and many others.

Mike Harris has covered my team for a number of years for the *Richmond Times-Dispatch*. He covered us when we didn't win too many games, and he covered us when we won all our games and played for the national championship. He's always impressed me by being thorough and fair. I know he put in the necessary time to make this a quality book. It shows with each of the stories he tells about 27 Tech athletes and the game of each of their lives. He's written with equal aplomb about some of the stars and some of the non-stars who had a memorable day.

There's not a Virginia Tech fan out there who won't find this book a great reading experience. If you attended one of the games, you'll get a kick out of reliving it along with one of your favorite Hokies. If you didn't attend the game, you'll feel like you did when you finish the chapter.

—Frank Beamer
Head football coach, Virginia Tech

FOOTBALL

CHAPTER 1

DICKIE BEARD

In 1996, Dickie Beard received a terrific Christmas present from daughter Diane, one of his four children. She put together two detailed scrapbooks of her father's exploits as a football player in high school, at Virginia Tech and in the military. It was quite a labor of love, and it is something Beard shows off with great pride these days.

"It was really special," Beard says of the gift. "It must have taken her a while to do it."

Photos, media guides, newspaper clippings, letters, and more make up the two thick books. It makes for very entertaining—and educational—reading. To see Virginia Tech described as "a little engineering" school, as it was at that time, would elicit a belly laugh from someone who has only seen the school in recent years. It's hardly little, with an enrollment of 28,000. And it's far more than an engineering school, though engineering is a large part of Tech's culture.

When Beard went there, though, the description was quite accurate. The school had an enrollment of just 3,000, and it was a long way from his Cumberland, Maryland, home. It was in Cumberland that Beard earned the nickname "The Cumberland Flash," because of his speed and prowess in both football and track. The Hokies had an "in" with Beard because his brother Ralph played at Tech in the 1940s. Ralph Beard scored the school's only touchdown in the 1946 Sun Bowl.

"We didn't get down to see him too much," Beard says of his brother's college playing days. "It was about an eight-hour drive and that was before

3

Interstate 81 was even thought about, so we'd only get down once or twice a year. I remember they played up this way once and we saw that game.

"I wasn't even planning on going anywhere on a football scholarship. I was so little. But I did good in high school and that got me thinking more about it. Tech recruited me. Maryland was after me some, that's when they had their big guns. I was familiar with Tech and I liked the school better than Maryland."

So The Cumberland Flash decided to follow in his brother's footsteps in Blacksburg, Virginia.

The Setting

Beard enrolled at Tech during an interesting time for the football squad. The Hokies competed in the Southern Conference, at the time a big, sprawling conference with an excellent reputation. (It's Division I-AA in football now.) In 1953, eight of the conference's schools split to form the Atlantic Coast Conference. Tech was not included. As *The Washington Post* wrote, it "got the brush off as too unimportant."

The snub didn't sit well with Tech, and remained in the school's consciousness for more than 50 years. When the ACC expanded recently, Tech was included, thanks in no small part to political pressure put on the University of Virginia to make sure the other Division I-A program in the state wasn't left behind. That didn't sit well with many in the ACC, who still didn't want Tech in the league. But Tech quickly showed it belonged by winning the 2004 ACC championship.

Beard said the 1954 team didn't know much about the goings-on that led to the formation of the ACC. He knows the exclusion of Tech was a hot topic at the school and he notes that the 2004 ACC title was Tech's first "official" championship. The 1954 team, he said, liked to consider itself the unofficial ACC champions.

"I don't know what all went on, but I know there were some hard feelings [because] they didn't take us in," Beard says. "We say we were the ACC champs that year. We won more ACC games than any of the ACC teams did."

Well, almost. Tech was 4-0 against ACC teams in 1954, the same record Duke and Maryland posted in league play. North Carolina also won four

Notes on Dickie Beard

Name:	Richard Vanmetre "Dickie" Beard
Born:	October 20, 1933
Hometown:	Cumberland, Maryland
Current residence:	Roanoke, Virginia
Occupation:	Retired. Ran his own janitorial service for 30 years. Now spends time with his four children and 13 grandchildren, all of whom live in the Roanoke area.
Position:	Halfback
Height/Playing weight:	5-8, 170
Years lettered:	1952-55
Accomplishments:	Beard led the Hokies in rushing three straight years, 1953-55, and finished his career with 1,378 yards on 280 carries. His best year was 1954, when he rushed 128 times and led the Southern Conference with 647 yards, 88 yards better than the runner-up. The Associated Press named him the state's outstanding athlete in 1954. He was also the Norfolk Sports Club's 1954 Most Valuable Player among state football players and a member of the All-Southern Conference team.
Nickname:	The Cumberland Flash
The game:	Virginia Tech at Clemson, October 2, 1954

league games, against two defeats. Tech's success against ACC teams was noticed around the league. A man named Jim Weaver was the ACC's commissioner at the time, an interesting fact given that a man named Jim Weaver was Tech's athletic director when the school finally gained admission to the league 50 years later. Weaver the commissioner was quoted before the Hokies' 1954 game at Clemson as saying, "The first thing you know, Tech will claim the ACC championship and then want a spot in the Orange Bowl."

The Hokies certainly weren't thinking bowls two games into the season. They just wanted to keep winning.

* * *

Dickie Beard apologizes. The game was a long time ago and he doesn't remember all that much. Yet he does remember one key thing about Virginia Tech's trip to Clemson in October of his junior season with the Hokies.

"It was hot—real hot, almost 100 degrees," Beard recalls. "We didn't have all that stuff they have today to help keep you cool. We really felt that heat."

Beard's team was hot on the field that day, figuratively hot before it even made the trip. The Hokies were in their fourth season under Frank Moseley, who hadn't posted a winning record in the first three. The 1954 team opened with victories against North Carolina State and Wake Forest. Its trip to Clemson was seen as a real test. Clemson was, as *The Washington Post* wrote, one of the big guys of college football. Tech was "the little engineering school sometimes called VPI." The two were not considered on the same level in football. Clemson and Tech had played four times over the previous 20 years, and Clemson had won all four with relative ease.

But the Hokies were convinced they were the better team in 1954, convinced the year was going to be something special. They went into Clemson and produced a first half that Moseley told reporters "was the best I've ever seen." Beard, enjoying the start of an all-Southern Conference season, was part of that. In the first half, he took a handoff deep in Clemson territory. Newspaper accounts vary. Some say he was 14 yards away, some say he was 18 yards away from the end zone.

"Let's go with 18," Beard says with a laugh. "Yeah, it was 18."

Dickie Beard followed his brother Ralph on the Virginia Tech football team.

Beard's memory of that day may be a little shaky, but luckily for the Hokies, their play was anything but.

Game Results

They left Clemson that hot day with an 18-7 victory. Beard did his part, scoring on that 18-yard run and picking up 74 yards on 17 carries. He also made several key tackles on defense. His kicking wasn't good that day, as he missed all three conversion attempts. But it hardly figured in the game's outcome.

"There wasn't any such thing as a specialist back then. I played halfback on both sides, plus I was the kicker," recalls Beard. "I was in high school when I started punting, kicking off, and doing extra points. Of course, there were many better punters than me when I was in college.

"There weren't as many guys on the team back in those days as there is now, but we had some real talent. George Preas [an offensive lineman] went on and played in the NFL for a long time. We had a real good team that year."

Later in the season, Tech defeated archrival Virginia, 6-0, to complete a 4-0 sweep of ACC teams. The only blemish the entire season was a 7-7 tie with William and Mary. The Hokies finished 8-0-1. No other Tech team went unbeaten during the regular season until the 1999 team finished 11-0.

"Coach Moseley was a real hard-nosed fellow," remembers Beard. "He believed in blocking and tackling and lots of running. This was not during games—this was after practice. I think we won some of those ballgames in 1954—and Clemson is one of them—just by being in better shape than the other teams. We just wore Clemson down in the second half."

Beard, Moseley told reporters later in the '54 season, "has been a lifesaver for us." Injuries affected the Hokies' depth in the offensive backfield and Beard had to carry more of a load than normal. He wound up leading the Southern Conference in rushing and the Hokies in scoring with 39 points. He missed those three conversions against Clemson, but he didn't miss too many others. He also intercepted three passes that season, tying him with Leo Burke for the team lead.

Life After Tech

Beard was inducted into Tech's Hall of Fame in 1987, the same year current coach Frank Beamer took over the program. The current Hokies are familiar to Beard, who has had season tickets with his wife, Wanda, since 1972. Beard goes to some road games, too, a much easier task now that the Hokies are in the ACC and play a number of road games within easy driving distance from his home in Roanoke, Virginia. Several of Beard's former teammates are regulars at most home games.

"We met a lot of people when I was at Tech, people I became lifelong friends with. It has been such a major thing in my life and we really enjoy following the team now," Beard says. "I like what Coach Beamer has done. He's been very good with Tech; he's very humble and he just looks after you.

"I don't remember a whole lot of the details anymore, but I remember we had some pretty good teams. I'm still in touch with some of the fellows. Tech was a good time in my life."

CHAPTER 2

CARROLL DALE

Carroll Dale grew up in the coal country of Wise, Virginia, where he still lives today. Even after a long and decorated career as a professional football player, Dale remains a small-town guy at heart.

"Oh yeah," he says. "That's the reason I was so happy in Green Bay. It was a small town. You can get across town in 15 minutes, no problem. I always loved the hills. Never have and never will care for the big city. Too much traffic. Even back when I was in Los Angeles, you could spend two hours trying to get 50 miles."

He was, quite simply, gifted. His athletic skills would have stood out anywhere. In a small town, they glared and screamed. Those skills got him a chance to do something he otherwise wouldn't have been able to do—go to college.

"My dad was a coal miner," says Dale, who worked for a while in the coal business himself after his pro career ended. "We had meager means, didn't even have a car until I was a sophomore in high school. And that was one car."

Times were different then, and Dale knew it would take a lot of hard work to gain entry to college.

"This was probably before they had all the financial aid that they have these days," Dale says of college. "I probably could not have gone [if not for sports]. When I was a junior and senior in high school, I knew I had to make the grades to play in high school, and that I needed the grades to get into college.

"I loved sports. When August 15 came around and we could start practicing football, it was like Christmas to me. Even though it was hard work, it was an exciting time."

When it came time to pick a college, Dale signed with the University of Tennessee. This was before the letter-of-intent became a binding agreement. The Southeastern Conference had such a rule, but it was only for conference schools.

"I visited Georgia Tech, Kentucky, and Tennessee," he recalls. "I signed with UT. Then I visited Clemson and Richmond and Virginia and Virginia Tech. Tennessee started feeding me some smoke about making All-America and all that stuff.

"Then I went up to Tech. Coach [Frank] Moseley said, 'We are going to offer you an opportunity to get an education and play all the football you want to play.' Blacksburg was a much better fit for me. I felt like I would have much less temptation there, and be able to concentrate on the books. Not having a vehicle, I could get downtown easily or get to church."

Dale wasted no time, choosing engineering as a focus and joining classes at Tech during the first summer session to get a leg up in math and english. On the football field, however, he was already way ahead of the curve.

The Setting

John Moody, who now works in athletic fund raising at Tech, played for the Hokies in 1952 and '53 before going into the service for two years. He came back to find his new partner at receiver.

"I went to high school in the Richmond area," Moody says. "We had really good football teams when I was in high school. But coming from little-bitty Wise County, we didn't have anybody with Carroll's talent. And we had a lot of good players.

"He did things so easy. He ran so smoothy it didn't look like he was doing anything. He was extremely fast, had great hands. I remember wind sprints. I made up for a lack of size with a lack of speed. Not Carroll. If we ran a 50-yard wind sprint, he'd beat us by 10 yards.

"If he was playing in today's football, he'd finish his career with 35, 40 touchdowns. He had that kind of talent, and he could play today."

Notes on Carroll Dale

Name:	Carroll Wayne Dale
Born:	April 24, 1938
Hometown:	Wise, Virginia
Current residence:	Wise, Virginia
Occupation:	Athletic fund raiser, University of Virginia-Wise
Position:	Split end
Height/Playing weight:	6-1, 195
Years lettered:	1956-59
Accomplishments:	Dale played in his first game at Tech as a non-starter then started the final 39 games of his career. He was Tech's first All-American and was the Southern Conference player of the year in 1958. He also won the Jacobs Blocking Trophy. He led the team in receiving each of his four seasons. Dale left Tech and had a long career in the National Football League, starting on three straight championship teams for the Green Bay Packers including the first two Super Bowl winners. His 205 receiving yards (on six catches) against Detroit on September 29, 1968 rank among the best single games in Packers history. He led Green Bay in catches from 1959-71. He is in the College Football Hall of Fame as a 1987 inductee.
The game:	Richmond at Virginia Tech, November 8, 1958

The ball didn't get thrown as much then as it does now. Though he led Tech all four years he was there, Dale's career numbers aren't spectacular: he caught 67 passes for 1,195 yards and 15 touchdowns.

"At that time, nobody had the wide-open offense in this area," Dale says. "Maybe out in Texas they were playing wide open. Not around here."

Dale didn't start his first game at Tech, though he did play thanks to some circumstances that took some veteran receivers off the team. But he started every other game in his career. He doubled as a defensive end and even jokes that he had a third position—tight end at lunchtime.

"When it comes down to who pays, then I'm a tight end," he says. "I was just fortunate enough to be in a position to play and I played most of those games for 60 minutes. I don't remember coming out much.

"Through necessity, they threw me in and I did well enough that they kept me in. I got an opportunity by chance. We're in the Sugar Bowl playing Tulane in the second game of the year, and I was starting. I didn't know enough to be nervous or scared. I just went out and played."

Dale only caught eight passes as a freshman, good enough for the team lead. It was the third straight year that the team leader had fewer than 10 catches. He more than doubled his total the next season with 17. As a junior, Dale caught 25 passes for six touchdowns, tying a Southern Conference record for scoring catches in a season.

* * *

These days, people would laugh if you talked about Richmond and Virginia Tech playing in a grudge football game. The Hokies are part of the game's elite, a consistent member of the Top 25 and owners of a bowl streak of 13 seasons. The Spiders have a fine program as well, but they're in Division I-AA now. The talent gap is wide, and the teams haven't played each other in 22 years.

It hasn't always been that way. The state of Virginia's "big five" used to consist of Tech, Virginia, William and Mary, Richmond, and Virginia Military Institute. The latter three schools are Division I-AA now, but in the "old days" the five were very competitive.

Carroll Dale, a budding star receiver at Tech, remembers a game against Richmond from his freshman season very well.

The small-town lifestyle at Virginia Tech suited Carroll Dale.

"We didn't even wear a single bar facemask," Dale says. "I remember there were 3-4 receivers that had to have stitches. There were a lot of elbows flying ... they beat up on us.

"My attitude was, somebody's playing dirty, they're the one's going to get caught. I didn't try to retaliate. If I had to block them, it would increase the motivation to do a good job. A little extra motivation doesn't hurt."

Tech got the ultimate revenge by winning that 1956 game 46-14, and by whipping the Spiders again the following year 42-7. When the Spiders came to visit for the 1958 season, it was a different deal. Tech has started the season 3-1 but lost badly at Florida State, dropped a one-point heartbreaker against West Virginia and then tied N.C. State. Plenty was riding on this game, and it turns out, a single pass to Dale.

Game Results

The Hokies trailed in the third quarter against Richmond. Tech quarterback Billy Holsclaw and Dale had already hooked up for one touchdown. This time, Dale hauled in a 37-yarder for his second score of the game. Tech lined up for the two-point conversion. Holsclaw dropped back and found his favorite target, Dale. But the pass was a little too long. Dale stretched and dove.

"Laying out and catching the ball is probably more of a natural ability," Dale says. "You see people dive for that ball. If they don't have the ability to turn while they are falling, they aren't going to make the catch. You have to be able to catch it and flip your shoulder over. Otherwise, as you come to the ground, the ball is going to be separated. Something has to hit the ground first besides the ball. Some guys can do that now, some guys can't. It has to be a motion of, dive, catch and turn."

The conversion pass from Holsclaw was indeed a tad long. Not a problem for a receiver with Dale's skills. He laid out, got his hands on the ball, hit the ground and held on. It was the best catch Dale made that year, and maybe in his collegiate career. Yet it didn't even count as an official catch, though it did give his team two valuable points.

Dale led Coach Frank Moseley's team in receiving all four seasons.

Wendy Weisend, writing in *The Techgram*, called the play "what is bound to be one of the finest receptions ever made in Miles Stadium on a diving, last-ditch grab."

Tech ended up winning the game, 27-23. Dale says he doesn't remember too many specifics of that game. "There's been a whole lot of football games played since then," he says of his playing career. But he did note that "as far as making catches, that was probably my best game."

Life After Tech

Dale follows sports now and stays in touch with a lot of his former teammates through golf outings. His NFL alumni team got to go to Phoenix last year for the Super Bowl of Golf, finishing fourth.

Golf may take up some of his free time, but it was football that opened a lot of doors for him. He received an education and the chance to win three Super Bowls playing for the legendary Vince Lombardi and the Green Bay Packers. Dale credits his success in football to his small-town upbringing.

"I think the real key is my homelife training, my background," Dale says. "I was taken to church, not sent. By having a higher purpose in life, spiritually speaking, I didn't put that total emphasis on sports. It was kind of an important thing that I loved to do. It wasn't the only reason for living. I really think the spiritual side of it kept me in line, trying to do the right thing."

Moody, Dale's teammate for two years, knew he was going to be a success with or without football.

"What an excellent work ethic," Moody says of Dale. "A great person, a great leader, a leader by example. He had great individual character. He was always going to class, always doing his homework, always had the Good Book with him. Whatever he did, whatever he does, it's going to get done the class way. As wonderful a player as he was, he's a better person."

CHAPTER 3

BOB SCHWEICKERT

Bob Schweickert's life turned in a football stadium. But it wasn't during a football game. As a 13-year-old, he went to what is now called University of Richmond Stadium to hear orator Billy Graham.

"When I was 13, I gave my life to the Lord at a Billy Graham crusade," Schweickert recalls. "I said this is what I want. I really accepted the Lord as my dad because I didn't have one.

"It's kind of the way I was. ... When I got to the Jets as a pro player, my nickname was 'Mother.' I was the mother of the guys ... that's the stand that I took, and that's just the way my whole life has been. I always talked to high schools and such, about Jesus and how important [religion] can be.

"When I met my wife—we're just crazy in love—the foundation in her life is her love of the Lord. We give God the glory; we give Him the glory in all of it. She has two wedding rings on her finger; the first one is from when she accepted the Lord and put Him first in her life. I come in second but, boy, coming in second is better than coming in first with most marriages."

As a young man, Schweickert was blessed with considerable athletic ability. Tommy Francisco, whose career at Tech overlapped Schweickert's by a year, called him "the best athlete I ever played with at Virginia Tech."

"I'll never forget as a freshman, him coming down the field in practice," remembers Francisco. "He just faked me out of my jock. He was fast and a real intelligent guy. Any time he went to class, he carried a football with him. You'd see him going across the drill field with that football in his arms."

Schweickert was just thrilled to be in college. His father left home when he was much younger. An older brother had gone to Tech, "and my mother had to do all she could to help him," says Schweickert. He wasn't sure during his days at Midlothian High School if he would be recruited by any school outside his immediate area.

"We were playing at Colonial Heights and I was having a pretty good game," Schweickert says. "An official came up to me and said, 'Son, where are you going to college?' I asked if he really thought I could go to college. I thought I was playing for Midlothian and nobody knew who I was. I was just doing the best I could.

"But by my senior year, I started getting phone calls from colleges, and I ended up with about 24 offers. I met with Coach [Jerry] Claiborne and I really liked Tech. I had to also think of when there would be an opportunity to play. Terry Strock was going to be a senior, so when I was a sophomore they would need a quarterback."

The job was ticketed for Schweickert, just the type of quarterback Claiborne loved. Since he didn't like to throw much, Claiborne preferred a quarterback who could scare people with his running ability. That was Schweickert.

The Setting

En route to taking over the quarterback job, Schweickert suffered a severe injury to his left shoulder.

"We were in practice and someone had stopped my progress and I was standing," Schweickert recalls. "Two of my teammates hit me as hard as they could and my shoulder socket split. That was as painful as anything. Coach Claiborne said, 'Get up, you have to play.' I said I could not. He told me I had to run up and down the sidelines until the end of practice.

"It was the most pain I had ever felt. Another kid had broken his arm at the same practice. They sent us to the doctor in Roanoke in a car. My left shoulder was broken, and his right arm was broken. He was shifting with his left arm, while I drove with my right. Imagine them doing that to [Michael] Vick.

"I got there and the fellow said to me, 'You'll be ready in 3-4 days.' I couldn't breathe, much less move. They sent the X-rays of my right shoulder,

Notes on Bob Schweickert

Name: Robert L. Schweickert

Born: September 17, 1942

Hometown: Richmond, Virginia

Current residence: Northbrook, Illinois

Occupation: Schweickert retired from the furniture business and he and wife Georgeanne are in the ministry.

Position: Quarterback

Height/Playing weight: 6-1, 191

Years lettered: 1962-64

Accomplishments: The Tech media guide describes Schweickert as "one of the finest triple-threat quarterbacks in the history of the Southern Conference." He was named to the 1964 All-America team by the Football Writers Association of America. He was the Southern Conference player of the year in 1963 when he ran for a record 839 yards and had a record 1,526 yards of total offense. He and fullback Sonny Utz combined for more than 6,000 yards of offense the three years they played together. Schweickert finished with 3,475 yards of total offense. He's among the school's all-time leaders in rushing, passing and total offense. Schweickert was inducted into the Tech Hall of Fame in 1983.

Nickname: The Bon Air Bullet

The game: Virginia Tech at Tulane, November 3, 1962

which was slightly separated. I asked, 'Why don't you go back and take X-rays of the left shoulder?'

"There was nothing they could do. ... I went in the shower every day and just about scalded myself. I would lift my arm [over and over]. Today I have no problem with my left shoulder, and I think that's because I did what I did and didn't leave it stationary."

Tech soldiered on without Schweickert, with Pete Cartwright at quarterback. It was shut out in two of its first four games, but did manage a one-point win over George Washington and a five-point victory over Virginia. Schweickert returned for the fifth game, though he wasn't effective in his first three games back. He had minus-11 rushing yards over that span as Tech lost two of the three.

"I never gave up when I was hurt," Schweickert says. "[But] when you are hit like that and your body gives ... you're going to have some question [as to] whether you can take another hit. It's like a guy with a knee that's torn out. He has to run and take some hits and gain some confidence. Initially, I was a bit tentative. I remember telling Coach Claiborne when he came to see me, 'Coach, I will give you all that I have. I hope that is good enough.'"

So it wasn't with any great confidence that the team headed to Tulane to play the Green Wave in the Sugar Bowl—the stadium, not the game.

"The one thing that really stands out is we needed to win," Schweickert recalls.

Game Results

Bob Schweickert's legs were burning. He was running as fast as he could and he wasn't certain he was getting anywhere. The end zone seemed like it was a long way away. The play had started back on Virginia Tech's 26-yard line. Tech was playing against Tulane, a small team going against a big team in a big stadium in a huge game.

"Tulane had a lot of meaning as a team," says Schweickert. "It was by far the largest stadium we had ever played in. ... It was a coliseum to us. It was one of the bigger teams we had played."

To that point, Tech was 3-4 and not enjoying the kind of season it expected. Schweickert needed a breakout day, his team needed a victory, and Tech was behind in the game. Schweickert, an option-style quarterback more

Bob Schweickert recovered from a severe injury to lead Virginia Tech to victory at Tulane.

dangerous as a runner than a passer, broke toward the sideline and turned upfield. With Green Wave defenders in hot pursuit, Schweickert kept going and going and going.

"I probably shouldn't admit this, but I do admit it," Schweickert says. "I was running down the sidelines with tears of joy streaming down my face. The joy of playing and helping a football team ... and we were going to win this football game."

They were going to win it if Schweickert got into the end zone. His legs still burned, but he kept running and running and running—74 yards in all to score the touchdown and complete the comeback. Tech won, 24-22, and Schweickert finally displayed what all the fuss was about when he enrolled.

"I was so happy to get into the end zone that I jumped up in the air and missed my feet and fell," he recalls with a laugh.

Dick Thompson, writing in the *Roanoke Times*, said Schweickert "cut down Green Wave defenders like wheat" on that long run. That wasn't all he did. Schweickert ran for an 11-yard touchdown and passed to Mike Cahill for another. He rushed for 143 yards and passed for 91. The 234 yards of total offense broke the 1958 school record Billy Holsclaw set against West Texas State.

"There are a couple of things that are still vivid to me from that game," remembers Schweickert. "One is that we almost never threw a dropback pass. I never threw a dropback pass in high school, never threw one at Virginia Tech, and never threw one with the Jets. I was always rolling out and throwing. I threw a 28-yarder in that game. I think it was the longest pass I'd ever thrown. I can still picture Mike Cahill going down and me throwing across the middle. We normally didn't do that."

Schweickert was also Tech's punter. He punted five times against Tulane and three of them went out of bounds on the 5-, 15-, and 16-yard lines.

"We were tremendously pleased with the performance by Bob Schweickert in his first full game on offense," Claiborne wrote in the November 5, 1962 edition of *Tech Sports*. "He certainly did an outstanding job of running and passing the football."

Schweickert's running ability was more important than his skills as a passer.

Reflecting on Tech

"I really believe Coach Claiborne probably should have redshirted me that year," Schweickert says. "They just needed a quarterback so bad. ... I would say that the victory by our team at Tulane was one of the things that helped me gain some confidence. We came from behind to win. We were kind of on our way at that point."

Tech finished 5-5 that season. The next two seasons, it won 14 of 20 games. The team was 8-2 in Schweickert's junior year, losing only at Kentucky and North Carolina State. Despite the slow start to his Tech career, Schweickert went on to earn numerous honors and awards—not to mention a pro career.

"Being selected as an All-American was a tremendous honor for a school like Virginia Tech and for me," Schweickert says. "It meant a lot and it means a lot—even today when someone introduces me as an All-American from Virginia Tech.

"Virginia Tech was a part of my foundation. Jesus is the main foundation. Virginia Tech happened to be part of my puzzle that fit together. My heart is with them in everything that they do.

"Virginia Tech is a part of Bob Schweickert. Bob Schweickert is a part of Virginia Tech."

Chapter 4

TOMMY FRANCISCO

Virginia Tech received the services of Tommy Francisco because it hid him out on a houseboat that belonged to Francisco's father. Recruiting was a different game back in the '60s, not as crazy in some ways as it has become, and yet more crazy in other ways. You could sign a letter of intent with one school and change your mind right up to the time practice started, so long as your "new" school and your "old" school weren't in the same conference.

A military child, Francisco was born in Mississippi but moved to the small Virginia town of Damascus when he was young.

"I spent all 12 years of school in one building," Francisco says. "We were the smallest school in the state of Virginia to field a football team."

Tech recruited him harder than anyone. He'd been going to games in Blacksburg for years and always figured he'd be a Hokie. But neither that nor the fact that he'd signed with Tech failed to sway Kentucky, and Francisco promised he'd take a visit there.

"I was easily swayed, and I signed with them," he says. "My mom and dad were so angry with me ... they were both battling for me right up to the last minute.

"My daddy had a houseboat back then and Tech came and took me out on that boat for three days until it was time to go to Tech. We just got out in the middle of the lake [and sat there]. I just loved to fish. I figured out later what was going on there."

What was going on was that Tommy's dad had his mind made up: Tommy was going to Tech.

The Setting

Tech coach Jerry Claiborne was putting together a solid program about the time Francisco arrived. The Hokies went 4-5 and 5-5 in Claiborne's first two seasons before posting an 8-3 record in his third, Francisco's first at the school. Records of 6-4 and 7-3 followed. Francisco's senior season was projected to be one of the Hokies' best, but it didn't start out that way. The team lost 13-0 at Tulane in its first game of the season.

"The heat about killed us," Francisco recalls. "Dickie Longerbeam [another offensive back] broke his neck and wasn't able to play the rest of the year."

After whipping George Washington 49-0 in the second game, the Hokies tied West Virginia 13-13 in their third. A 1-1-1 start wasn't what anyone envisioned. But things turned from there. The Hokies were involved in a number of close games the rest of the way and won them all. They beat Kentucky 7-0, defeated Florida State 23-21, and dropped Wake Forest 11-0 and William & Mary 20-18.

Going into its final game of the year against VMI, that left Tech at 7-1-1—and without a bowl bid. Bids weren't as plentiful then as they are now. Florida State, which lost to Tech, was going to a bowl, and the Hokies were not happy.

"We had such a great record. Florida State got the Sun Bowl bid with a 5-4 record," Francisco says. "That's what we were really so upset about."

And someone had to pay the price for that.

Game Results

VMI had beaten Claiborne's first two teams, and would win again over Tech in 1967. For a while, though, it was a one-sided series. Tech won 35-20 in 1963, 35-13 in 1964, and 44-13 in 1965. Yet even those relatively easy wins couldn't prepare people for the lopsided 70-12 thumping the Hokies gave the Keydets in 1966. The result left Claiborne defending himself and his team afterward.

"I didn't tell them to run up the score, but I didn't tell them to lie down either," Claiborne said in a *Roanoke Times* article that bore the headline *VMI Whipping Boy For Mad Gobblers*. "I'm certainly not ever going to tell a team

Notes on Tommy Francisco

Name:	Thomas Paul Francisco
Born:	March 16, 1945
Hometown:	Greenville, Mississippi
Current residence:	Fall Branch, Tennessee
Occupation:	Event coordinator for Professional Affairs. He sells company picnics, sometimes for thousands of people, and goes to them to make sure all runs smoothly.
Position:	Tailback
Height/Playing weight:	6-1, 190
Years lettered:	1964-66
Accomplishments:	By scoring six touchdowns in this game against VMI, Francisco broke a 44-year-old single-game record and it still stands today. He scored 14 touchdowns in that 1966 season to set a record that stood until Lee Suggs shattered it with 28 in 2000. His career touchdown total matched his jersey number—22—and Francisco still ranks among Tech's all-time scoring leaders with 134 points. Francisco's 203 carries in 1966 were a school record, and he finished the season with 753 yards. He had 1,555 career yards on 366 carries. Francisco had three games with at least 100 rushing yards.
Nickname:	Touchdown Tommy
The game:	Virginia Military Institute versus Virginia Tech in Roanoke, November 24, 1966

not to score. They wanted the points and they went out and got them. They never let up, hitting just as hard at the end as at the beginning. Even the reserves we put in there—and we played 47 men—didn't let down."

Francisco scored on runs of 1, 26, 1, 3, 1, and 3 yards. That's six touchdowns. He finished the day with 32 carries for 132 yards.

"He didn't have great speed, but he had good speed," recalls Frank Beamer, Tech's current head coach who was a safety on that 1966 team. "We were a good running football team and we started handing balls to him and kept on handing them to him and he kept going into the end zone."

Francisco didn't know he had broken the school record for touchdowns scored in a game until afterward. He just knew he wanted his final game to be one of his best.

"I was just thinking about it [being] my last college game at Virginia Tech. We weren't going to a bowl, and I wanted it to be a good game. Being my last game, I even mentioned to Coach Claiborne that I'd like to play more. He was really close with the seniors. Like all the coaches now, they really believe the senior leadership is important to the team."

Senior leadership aside, Claiborne might have sat Francisco more in the game if Tech been healthier.

"The only reason I got the six touchdowns was no one knew the plays," he says today. "The number two and three guys got hurt. I was in there playing with some guys who had never played in a game before.

"A lot of people thought we were running up the score. The thing I really remember is our defense just killed them. They didn't get a first down until the half was almost over. … We had two onside kicks that we recovered. We got some bad press for that. Coach Claiborne had an explanation for it: We just didn't have a whole lot of plays."

Despite the drubbing of VMI, Francisco was a dejected young man as he walked off the field at Victory Stadium following the final regular-season game of his senior season. On one hand, that was hard to understand after setting a school single-game record that still stands and leading Tech to an excellent mark of 8-1-1. But Francisco and his Hokie teammates were all dressed up with nowhere to go. The Hokies hadn't been invited to a bowl, and they left the field that day thinking their season was over.

That was hard on Francisco, who loved to play football and really wanted one more day. The thought that he was done bothered him as he

Tommy Francisco's 1966 record of six rushing touchdowns in a game still stands.

trudged off the field. Like his teammates, he headed home for a belated Thanksgiving meal. While on break, however, the Hokies received news worthy of thanks: The Liberty Bowl ended up inviting Tech to play against Miami.

In the game, Francisco scored Tech's only touchdown on a first-quarter, 1-yard run. The result wasn't what Tech had hoped for, as it fell 14-7. Francisco gained only 55 yards on 21 carries. Still, it was more than anyone else gained on the ground on a cold day in Memphis, Tennessee.

Reflecting on Tech

Francisco wore his Tech uniform a couple of times after that, participating in some postseason all-star games. Today, he keeps a memento from one of those all-star games in his home office.

"I have my helmet where I can see it, and there's some green paint on it," he says. "That's where Bubba Smith of Michigan State nailed me. He went on to have a pretty good pro career."

Though his playing days are long over and he's a grandfather now, Francisco looks back on his time at Tech as some of the best days of his life. Every year in January, players who played under Claiborne get together for a reunion in Myrtle Beach, South Carolina. During the 2006 season, the 1966 and '68 Liberty Bowl teams of Jerry Claiborne will have a reunion at Tech's home game against Cincinnati.

"I really enjoy the get-togethers," Francisco says. "We're getting up there [in age], and some of my buddies are dying on me.

"We had a winning record every year I played there. You work so hard. The closeness, the camaraderie you develop with the fellows you played with is amazing."

Looking back on his life after Tech, Francisco does have one regret.

"I love what I do now; I really enjoy my job," he says. "But to be honest, I've often regretted not trying coaching. Some of my good friends from when I played enjoyed their careers so much. The guy who was my best friend in college, Milt Miller, he won a state championship in Sylvester, Georgia, then went to the 4A level and won two more. I've often been envious of their careers.

Injuries prevented Francisco from possibly having a pro career for his coaching buddies to envy.

"I got drafted by Denver, but a knee injury kind of ended that before it got started," he recalls. "I just played in some exhibition games. I came back and tried to play for the Wheeling [West Virginia] Ironmen. I finished my knee off there.

"My right shoulder was separated one year and it hangs lower than the other one. I have arthritis in it. So I'm a little banged up. My wife can't understand how I'd say I'd do it all over again. But I would."

For Francisco, there's no feeling in the world like being out on a football field.

"I was at Tech's game against Boston College when Mike Imoh ran back the kickoff," he says. "I'd had the record for most kickoff returns and they announced he broke it. ... It reminded me that there's no feeling like it, when you're out there waiting for that kickoff, there's nothing like it at all."

CHAPTER 5

FRANK BEAMER

As head coaches on the collegiate level go, Frank Beamer is about as easy to deal with as any of them. One of the things that makes him so successful is that he doesn't worry about a lot of petty things that drive other coaches crazy. The media is not seen as the enemy, as a problem to be dealt with by expending as little effort as possible. Beamer welcomes reporters to every one of his practices. They can talk to him, to his assistant coaches, to the support personnel, to the players. He actually seems to enjoy their company, or at least he's a good pretender.

"He is as comfortable with himself as any coach as I've ever been around," says Kevin Rogers, one of Beamer's assistant coaches from 2002-2005.

Beamer talks easily on just about any subject. But one that he doesn't talk about as much is Frank Beamer the football player. He'll crack wise, make jokes about himself. He'll offer a line or two about his playing days, but swears he doesn't remember much detail. Good thing his former teammates do.

The Setting

Mike Widger calls Beamer, the player, a "tough son of a gun."

"He came to play every day," continues Widger, a linebacker and leader of Tech's defense in 1968. "Frank was just a piece of work. He did things on the field that a 5 feet, 10 inch cornerback shouldn't do. Our whole defensive backfield was like that. They were all the same size, and they were all hitters. Back then, we lived on defense. We didn't have an offense."

A childhood accident left Beamer no choice but to be tough. When he was seven years old, an explosion in a barn on the family's property left him severely burned. Tough love came from his mother, Herma Beamer, a schoolteacher who helped her son through the ordeal, but didn't let him feel sorry for himself or learn to the definition of the word "quit." That drive propelled Beamer to become a good athlete.

His family lived about an hour away from Tech, so he followed the Hokies as well as Wake Forest.

"I remember coming up here with my uncle. We'd come to see Bob Schweickert play," Beamer says. "I was a big fan of Schweickert.

"Things just kind of worked out for me. At the time, Tech was recruiting about 60 guys, and I don't know where I was on the pole. I never actually took a recruiting visit. They called me up and said they were going to offer me a scholarship, and I told them I'd accept. I didn't want to give them a chance to back out. So that all worked out."

Beamer describes himself as a consistent player who didn't make many mistakes.

"I think I had that football sense," he says. "I don't think I had the size or the athletic ability that some had but, I felt like I could get myself to the right place at the right time."

On at least one occasion in 1968, that much was true.

Game Results

The pass by University of Richmond quarterback Buster O'Brien headed straight toward Frank Beamer, who knew before the pass fell into his hands that the potential on this one was great. He could see plenty of open field in front of him, right down to the end zone.

"It was coverage where I had the freedom to come back inside. I didn't have deeper responsibility," Beamer says. "Buster kind of rolled his eyes and let it go, and I intercepted it."

He hadn't scored a touchdown as a result of any of his previous interceptions. This "pick" was Beamer's chance. With the ball safely in his grasp, Beamer took off toward the promised land of the end zone. Snow was

Notes on Frank Beamer

Name:	Frank Beamer
Born:	October 18, 1946
Hometown:	Hillsville, Virginia
Current residence:	Blackburg, Virginia
Occupation:	Head football coach, Virginia Tech
Position:	Cornerback
Height/Playing weight:	5-10, 155
Years lettered:	1966-68
Accomplishments:	A three-year starter, Beamer finished his career with nine interceptions, leading the team with four as a sophomore in 1966. He went on to greater fame as a collegiate coach, winning 42 games in six years at Murray State before taking over at his alma mater. Starting with the 1993 season, Beamer led the Hokies into a bowl game every year. They played for the national championship after the 1999 season, losing to Florida State in the Sugar Bowl.
The game:	Richmond at Virginia Tech, November 9, 1968

falling. Wind was blowing. He was moving as fast as he could, which he's always said isn't very fast.

Beamer was left with one man to beat, the man who had thrown the ball that he was now holding.

"Buster was a great quarterback," Beamer recalls. "Had a great arm and could really throw the ball. But he was, well, kind of slow.

"I got inside the 10, to the five and I thought, 'Man, he's going to catch me.'"

But O'Brien never did catch Beamer, who managed to get into the end zone for the only touchdown of his collegiate career.

"He had an angle on me. I have this picture somewhere, he's just diving at me," Beamer says. "And I'm going into the end zone.

"After I scored that touchdown, I flipped the ball right into the stands. You know that statement, 'Act like you've been there?' Well, I hadn't been there and I was so excited to get there, I still don't know why, I just threw [the ball] up there. ... It wasn't against the rules when I did it. I don't think much was made of it back then."

Tech ended up beating the Spiders 31-18, thanks in no small part to Beamer's 50-yard touchdown with 8:54 left in the third quarter. In his account of the game for *Tech Sports*, writer Newton Spencer referred to Beamer as "little defensive back Frank Beamer." Jerry Claiborne, Tech's head coach at the time, was quoted afterward as saying, "The biggest play of the game was Beamer's interception because that really took the pressure off."

Beamer, the team's holder, also completed a 9-yard pass on a fake field goal. So it was a big day for the little defensive back, even if his teammates don't remember as much.

"He scored a touchdown? I don't remember that," says Widger, who scored two of his own that season on interception returns.

These days, a Tech victory over Richmond is expected. Those days it was anything but automatic. The 1968 loss to Tech was the only defeat the Spiders suffered in their final nine games that season. They closed the year by beating Ohio in the Tangerine Bowl, leaving them ranked 18th in the final United Press International Poll and 20th in the final Associated Press poll.

Frank Beamer made up for a lack of physical gifts with a great mental approach to football.

Tech finished 7-4 in '68 and got into the Liberty Bowl, helped along by the victory over Richmond that was helped along by Beamer's interception and touchdown.

"Times have changed today with Division I-A and Division I-AA, but back then all the schools in the state like us and Virginia and Richmond and VMI and William and Mary, we were all on equal footing," Beamer says. "That was a real good win for us. Richmond had a great team with some awfully good players."

* * *

As much as Beamer enjoyed the touchdown that frigid November day in 1968, the best part of Beamer's day came later. He had a blind date that night with a woman from Richmond named Cheryl Oakley.

It must have gone well. She's now Cheryl Beamer.

Life After Tech

"I never really thought about coaching until my senior year was over, and I got to thinking about what I was going to do the next year. I didn't want to give up football, so I went back and took some more math classes so I could teach math in the Radford city school system and coach football.

"Deep down, I think I knew I always wanted to be around football."

Beamer worked his way up the coaching chain and eventually back to Tech. He coached in high school, then worked as a graduate assistant. Climbing the ladder proved to be worth the pain, but the process didn't happen without a fair amount of doubt.

"There were times I'd go home and say I didn't want to do this any more, that I couldn't take things the way they were going," Beamer says. "And my wife would say, 'What else are you going to do?' I really didn't have many options.

"Things have worked out, I've been very lucky in that regard."

Luck hasn't had as much to do with it as hard work. Over his years in coaching, Beamer has developed a fondness for players who value hard work—players who are a lot like Beamer.

Beamer has since gone on to great fame and acclaim as Virginia Tech's head coach.

"Actually," Beamer jokes, "I like for them to be a lot bigger and a lot faster than I was."

After six years as the head coach at Murray State, Beamer returned to his alma mater for the 1987 season. His early years at Tech were not good. After a 2-8-1 season in 1992, many Tech fans wanted Beamer gone. Fortunately, Tech's athletic director at the time didn't listen. Dave Braine liked Beamer's work ethic. He knew that Beamer took over the Hokies at a difficult time, when the school was digging out of a mess left by previous athletic director and coach Bill Dooley. And Beamer was loyal, turning down a chance to move to Boston College two years earlier.

Braine placed his faith in Beamer, and it paid off big. The Hokies haven't missed a bowl game since. Beamer has collected a number of coach of the year trophies, including one from the Atlantic Coast Conference after the 2004 and 2005 seasons. In their first year in the league, the Hokies were picked to finish sixth. They won the championship, perhaps Beamer's best coaching job on a resume fit for a Hall of Famer.

CHAPTER 6

MIKE WIDGER

When the greats of Virginia Tech football are discussed, a listener can tell who are the true diehards among Hokies fans. They'll mention the name Mike Widger.

Widger sometimes flies under the radar. One of his teammates was Frank Beamer, who is now the head coach at Tech. Another was Frank Loria, a standout on the field whose promising coaching career was cut short by a horrible tragedy, the Marshall University plane crash in 1970.

Big teammates aren't the only reason Widger is sometimes forgotten. Widger played pro ball, but his entire career was spent north of the border in Canada. He logged nine years playing for Montreal and Ottawa. So the acclaim that comes from playing in the National Football League never came to him.

Bigger names came before him, bigger names followed. Yet though the names were bigger, the players might not have been better.

"He kind of had an uncanny ability," says Beamer, who roomed with Widger for two years. "He wasn't an imposing linebacker. He was very athletic, and he just had a great knack of being at the right place at the right time.

"The words 'football instincts' probably fit him better than just about anybody I know. I remember one ballgame, he ripped the ball out of the running back's hands and took it all the way to the end zone. He just had that knack for making big plays, for being around the football."

The Setting

Widger ended up at Tech for the oddest of reasons. Undersized in high school, he didn't draw much attention from recruiters. Rutgers in his home state of New Jersey wanted him, and was ready to offer him a scholarship. Before accepting, Widger took a visit to Tech with his high school coach Lou D'Angelo.

"We went in and saw coach Jerry Claiborne. I was only 165 pounds then, and I was a center and a linebacker," Widger recalls. "Coach D'Angelo came out after I met with Coach Claiborne and he said, 'You got your scholarship.' I asked why. Coach D'Angelo said, 'Coach Claiborne liked you. He said you were bowlegged, [and] bowlegged people don't have knee problems.' That's how I got my scholarship—it was that simple."

Tech would find out later the bowlegged kid could play a little, too.

After a 7-3 record in 1967, Tech was primed for a big season in 1968. It started out slowly, with losses in three of the first five games. But the Hokies started to play better, knocking off Florida State on the road to even their record, and then beating Richmond at home in a game where Beamer scored the only touchdown of his collegiate career.

Up next was a difficult road trip to South Carolina. By that time, Widger was starting to get some notice.

"There may not be a better linebacker in the country, and Widger goes about proving it every weekend," Jerry Lindquist wrote in the *Richmond Times-Dispatch* three days before the game at South Carolina. When that article appeared, Widger wasn't sure he'd be able to play against South Carolina. He'd been in a hospital for two days, thanks to a problem with canker sores.

"I had no idea if I'd even be able to play," says Widger. "I couldn't eat all week. But somehow we managed to get things together, and I was able to get down there."

Widger flew down separately from the team, making it in time for kickoff.

Notes on Mike Widger

Name:	Michael John Widger
Born:	August 21, 1948
Hometown:	Pennsville, New Jersey
Current residence:	Pennsville, New Jersey
Occupation:	Retired. Widger worked a variety of jobs in several different countries after a nine-year pro career in Canada. Among the places he worked were Saudi Arabia and Egypt. "I've been up and down a lot of different streets," Widger said.
Position:	Linebacker
Height/Playing weight:	6-0, 196
Years lettered:	1967-69
Accomplishments:	In his junior season of 1968, Widger became a first-team All-America on teams selected by The Associated Press and the Football Writers Association of America. He intercepted seven passes and had 203 return yards. Two of his interceptions went for touchdowns. He scored another when he pulled the ball out of a runner's arms. Widger intercepted three more passes as a senior. His 12 career interceptions rank him sixth on Tech's all-time list. The school didn't start keeping tackling records until 1974. Widger surely would have been on those lists had they been kept when he played.
The game:	Virginia Tech at South Carolina, November 16, 1968

Game Results

It was a rainy, dreary night, but for Tech fans, it was a good night. For Widger, too. But one person in particular wasn't enjoying himself on the eve of November 16, 1968: South Carolina quarterback Tommy Sugg.

"I remember the surprised look on Suggs' face the first time that I blitzed. It was like he was wondering, 'Where the hell are you from?'" Widger recalls.

Widger finished the night with 15 unassisted tackles and 14 assists. As Widger remembers it, nobody could block him. Five of his tackles were sacks of Suggs, good for losses totaling 41 yards. Tech ended up with a 17-6 victory on the soggy night, "and then they flew me right back [to the hospital]," Widger recalls.

South Carolina and its fans probably wished Widger wouldn't have been allowed to leave the hospital in the first place. Over 40,000 fans looked on as Widger took down Suggs time and time again.

"Suggs was a guy who you'd probably compare to Doug Flutie," Widger says. "He was about the same size and he could throw the ball. ... But on that night, it was like nobody could block me."

Sports Illustrated agreed, naming Widger its national lineman of the week. Meanwhile, Tech went on to win its final two regular-season games and advanced to the Liberty Bowl, where it lost to Mississippi.

"We were playing Ole Miss and Archie Manning was the quarterback," says Widger. "We started out at the end of the first quarter ahead 17-0, and we lost the game 34-17.

"We'd seen a tendency—in 10 games they'd never run to the boundary side [short side]. They put the formation in and ran to the wide side. We shifted to the wide side and stunted to the wide side the whole first half. At halftime, I told Coach Claiborne and John Devlin, the linebackers coach, they were going to hurt us [and start going] to the boundary. Coach said we'd do it until they hurt us.

"First play of the second half, they put the formation to the wide side and go to the weak side, and 79 yards later it's thank you very much.

"Another thing I remember, they got to the 1-yard line three times and didn't get into the end zone in 12 plays. On the last one, Manning came

Mike Widger was named *Sports Illustrated*'s national lineman of the week after a victory over South Carolina.

down on the option and I stepped across the goal line and dropped him. He got up like he thought he scored. But he didn't."

The loss was disappointing, but overall Widger had enjoyed a heck of a year.

"That was my best year, my junior year," he remembers. "I had seven interceptions and three touchdowns. It was a whole lot of fun."

Widger was the Hokies' ringleader. In a letter sent to drum up support for Widger on All-America teams, Tech sports information director Wendy Weisend wrote, "He hasn't had a bad game—hasn't missed a play—and has been some kind of fantastic."

The Associated Press and Football Writers Association of America took note, naming Widger a first-team All-America. But even with the accolades and momentum, Widger's senior season proved a frustrating one. Claiborne was a defense-oriented coach, which was great for a defender like Widger. But it was not as great, Widger thinks, for the bottom line. In Widger's senior season, the Hokies fell to 4-5-1. After another losing season in 1970, Claiborne was gone despite the string of winning seasons from 1963-68.

"If we had an offensive coach when I was in college, we would have done a lot better than we did," Widger says. "My senior year, we lost the first four to five games because we couldn't put any points on the board. [Tech started 0-5 and put 10 or fewer points up in three of the games.] That was Jerry Claiborne football—his whole thing was defense. He wouldn't throw the ball.

"Going into my senior year, they brought Raymond Berry down to coach the receivers. He looked at the playbook and [said], 'What the hell am I here for? There's no reason for me to be here. You don't have an offense, it's that simple.' And we didn't."

Life After Tech

Widger thought his opportunity for playing time as a pro was better in Canada, so he headed there for nine years before embarking on a post-football career that took him overseas. He gets back to Tech once in a while and keeps up with his old roommate, Coach Beamer, by watching games on television.

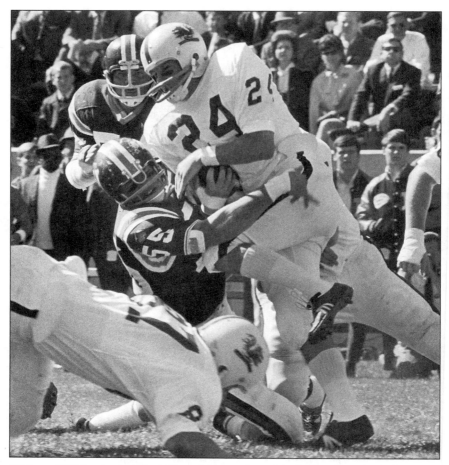

Widger (55) had a total of 29 tackles against South Carolina, including five sacks.

"[If I could], I'd go out tomorrow and play again," claims Widger. "I just liked playing the game. I would have paid them to let me play. I lost my front teeth eight times. But that didn't matter. That's small stuff. I enjoyed my experience at Tech, had a hell of a good time and met a lot of fine people.

"In the end, I got the trophies and everything. They're up in the attic—that's all incidental to me. That doesn't mean anything. I just played because I enjoyed doing it. ... I'd do it all over again and not change anything."

CHAPTER 7

DON STROCK

Don Strock took the snap from center and dropped back to pass, something he was doing a lot of these days much to his delight. Head coach Charlie Coffey and offensive coordinator Dan Henning had installed an offense at Virginia Tech that was in stark contrast to that of Coffey's predecessor, Jerry Claiborne. That was the coach who recruited Strock, and he believed in a strong running game and a stronger defense.

In 10 seasons under Claiborne, the most passes attempted by a quarterback in any season was 132. Twice, the quarterback didn't even get to 100. Strock, in his first season running the Coffey-Henning offense, threw 356 times. You need three heavy passing seasons under Claiborne to get that many.

If not for the arrival of Coffey and Henning, Strock might not have gotten a real shot at Tech. Strock's former teammate Mike Burnop jokes, "[Strock] owes his whole career to Dan Henning." All kidding aside, Strock agrees with that logic, saying that the new coaching duo "definitely opened the doors" for him. Yet Strock still has a lot of appreciation for what Claiborne taught him, and for that fact that Claiborne redshirted him a season.

"That turned out to be a blessing, because I had that extra year when we started throwing," Strock says. "Jerry Claiborne was a very tough guy. He had very physical practices, he taught you what it was all about. It was kind of a wakeup call for a freshman. We didn't throw the ball a lot, it was a different perspective."

Strock was a good enough athlete that he received scholarship offers to play basketball. Wake Forest wanted him. "I was one of those guys who jumped center and played guard," he says. It was Claiborne's style to recruit athletic quarterbacks because he knew they were generally pretty smart and he could play the ones who didn't win the quarterbacking spot at other positions. So Strock fit right in.

The Setting

The new Tech coaches thought they had the ingredients necessary to throw the ball more. When Coffey and Henning got a good look during their first spring, they received all the affirmation they needed.

"Don played his butt off," Burnop recalls. "He had an unbelievable arm and he was so tall. He had that great arm and great vision and a really good command of the offense, of what Henning wanted him to do."

Says Strock: "We saw how good [our new offense] could be, how productive it could be, and everybody kind of jumped on board."

Strock threw for 2,577 yards as a junior. In the previous 12 seasons, Tech's passing leader had never even hit the 1,000-yard mark. The Hokies put up some points—the 249 they scored that season were more than they'd had in any season under Claiborne. But so, too, were the 272 points Tech surrendered. Only one of Claiborne's teams gave up more than 200. Tech finished 4-7 in Coffey's first season.

Tech gave up another 253 points in 1972, but countered by scoring 307. Still, the improvement wasn't obvious in terms of record; Tech stood at 1-2 when Houston came to visit. The previous year, Tech had made a trip to the Astrodome to face Houston in a shootout Houston won 56-29. Now, the Cougars were repaying the favor by making a trip to Blacksburg.

"I'm pretty sure they had to change the light bulbs in the Astrodome scoreboard after that game," said Burnop, who as the Hokies' tight end caught a then-record 46 passes in 1971.

After getting an eyeful of Strock the year before, Houston still wasn't sure how to slow the Hokies. Strock was still passing and passing and passing. He'd finish the year with 427 attempts.

Notes on Don Strock

Name:	Donald Joseph Strock
Born:	November 27, 1950
Hometown:	Pottstown, Pennsylvania
Current residence:	Miami, Florida
Occupation:	Head football coach, Florida International University. Strock is the school's first football coach.
Position:	Quarterback
Height/Playing weight:	6-5, 205
Years lettered:	1970-72
Accomplishments:	Until Bryan Randall broke a lot of them in 2004, almost all the passing records at Virginia Tech belonged to Strock. He threw for 2,577 yards in 1971 and 3,243 in 1972, and finished with 6,009 career yards. His 53 attempts against Houston in 1972 remain a school record, as do his 34 completions and 527 yards in that game. He also shares the record for most interceptions in a game with five. Strock's 1972 yardage total led the nation. He remains the only Tech quarterback to ever throw for 3,000 yards in a season. Strock was a third-team All-America choice in 1972.
The game:	Houston at Virginia Tech, October 7, 1972

Game Results

Strock threw 52 times that day. He completed 34 of those passes for 532 yards. Burnop was on the other end of eight of the passes for 117 yards.

"That year, we came out firing from the first game," Strock recalls. "We had excellent receivers, we were well coached in the passing game. We had to make believers out of everybody. A guy comes in and says we're going to throw 35 times a game and we're all saying, 'Yeah, yeah, we don't throw it 35 times a year.' Once we got adjusted, everybody loved it.

"I don't think Houston had ever seen a passing team like ours before. One play, they didn't even have a middle linebacker. We just released the tight end inside—that was Mike [Burnop]—and popped him for 8, 10 yards at a time. They were a little discombobulated about how to cover a team like that, and we took advantage.

"What stands out to me is we threw for all those yards, and I don't think I threw for a touchdown. When we got down [close to the end zone], we went to a power game and tried to run in for all those touchdowns. ... We were able to go from the 20 to 20 pretty easily. I think we would have won the game if we had kept throwing the ball."

The Hokies ended up with a 27-27 tie. James Barber, the team's leading rusher in 1971 and 1972, fumbled six times. Tech lost three of them. It still would have won had it not missed an extra point in the fourth quarter.

Strock's 527 yards were 17 short of a single-game NCAA record set in 1968 by Greg Cook of Cincinnati.

"I was always pretty confident," says Strock. "I knew I could throw if I had the chance. I think what that game might have done is changed some of the players' mindsets, led them to think, 'Hey, if we can do it against these guys, we can do it against anybody.'

"Everybody was amazed you could throw for that many yards in one game. I think it opened the eyes of a lot of people. I just wish we'd been able to win the game. We finished [the season] 6-4-1, and 7-4 might have been good enough to get us in the bowl picture.

"But it was still a good game. A lot of people noticed it."

Don Strock was better known for his career as an NFL backup than he was as a Hokie.

Life After Tech

Flash forward 34 years. Mike Burnop is now the color commentator on Virginia Tech football and basketball broadcasts. Even though he's in his 50s, Burnop looks as if he can still get out there and play football. That's because he works out regularly.

One day he stopped in at Tech's Cassell Coliseum to get in a workout on a treadmill. A television was on in the room, tuned to ESPN Classic. The channel was replaying an NFL game between the Chargers and the Dolphins, featuring his old teammate, Don Strock.

Strock was drafted in the fifth round by the Miami Dolphins, and he stayed with them until 1987, becoming perhaps the most famous backup quarterback ever. On January 2, 1982, in a playoff game against San Diego—the same one that had caught Burnop's eye on the television—Strock came on in relief with Miami down 24-0. The Dolphins eventually lost the marathon game in overtime, 41-38. Both Strock and San Diego quarterback Dan Fouts threw for more than 400 yards.

"Watching that game made me think again about how good [Strock] could have been if he'd had the chance to start regularly in that league," Burnop says. "He was a big part of how good Dan Marino was in Miami because Don was such a coach-on-the-field type for all that time. It was unfortunate that he got drafted by such a quality team. He never really got a shot."

When his pro career ended after 17 seasons, Strock got away from football for a while. He served as a host at the Doral Country Club in Miami, Florida, for a while. A friend who started an Arena Football League team asked Strock to coach. He went from Arena Football to the World League to the NFL as an assistant, before becoming Florida International's first head coach.

"I enjoy coaching the young men," Strock says. "We're only in our fourth year of playing games. We're the fastest team to go from Division I-AA to I-A in the history of college football."

Strock still finds the time to keep up with his alma mater, and has been on the sidelines when Tech has played at Miami.

"I'm still a Hokie at heart," Strock says.

CHAPTER 8

RICK RAZZANO

Who knew that Joe Namath had a hand in recruiting Rick Razzano to Virginia Tech? Razzano didn't even know himself until several years ago, well after his days as a Hokie were over. A stellar high school career didn't garner Razzano much attention from recruiters, who pegged him too small and too slow. Only the University of Cincinnati was willing to offer a scholarship to the 5 feet, 11 inch, 225-pound middle linebacker.

"I was 50 minutes away from the University of Pittsburgh, and they never recruited me," Razzano says. "I got two offers to go on trips to Purdue and Indiana. Indiana's coach at the time was Lee Corso. Both brought me in and tried to show me a good time. On Sunday, that's when the coaches brought you into the office and talked to you. [Neither offered] me a scholarship because of my lack of size and my lack of speed."

Despite his lack of offers, Razzano was not enamored with playing for Cincinnati. What he didn't know at the time was that the wheels were turning elsewhere. Jimmy Sharpe, a former coach and player at Alabama, had taken over as head coach at Virginia Tech. He called Namath, another former Alabama player, and asked for the name of Namath's high school coach. Sharpe then called that coach, Larry Bruno, and asked about overlooked players in his area. Razzano was at the top of that list.

"That's how it started," says Razzano, who learned the full story while having dinner with his former coach four years ago. "He called me, recruited me. When I went down [to Virginia Tech] I thought it was just beautiful. It was everything I was looking for, except for being eight hours away from home. I fell in love with it, with the coaching staff."

That Tech was willing to take a chance on a smaller, slower player meant a lot to Razzano, who managed to have a fulfilling prep, college, and pro career despite his lack of size and speed.

"The game has always been based on leverage, and always will be based on leverage," he says. "Unfortunately, a lot of coaches like to look at their roster and see height and weight. There's a lot of guys out there like me who end up being overachievers. They have to work for everything, have to put in the extra effort because they know they don't have some of the tangible things the people at the next level are looking for. They work extra hard to excel at the areas they could excel in.

"It's the production on the field that counts, not how tall you are. We had one guy I was competing against [who] was a specimen. He was 6 feet, 4 inches, 240 pounds, and could run. He just couldn't play. But he looked good, no question."

It also helped, Razzano says, that he was going in with a new staff at Tech, much like he did with the Cincinnati Bengals years later.

"Whenever you go into a program where it is a brand-new staff, it gives everybody an equal playing field," Razzano says. "The second year I was in Cincinnati, those rookies had no chance."

The Setting

Razzano describes himself as a "quick study," and it must be true. He was recruited as a fullback and linebacker, and thinks Tech was thinking fullback first. That's how he ended up with No. 38.

His first glance at the defensive depth chart was unsettling: He was seventh team. But just two weeks later, he had advanced all the way to first team, where he stayed for four years.

"I guess they saw something good in my ability to play," he says. "I've had a lot of coaches over the years. Our defensive coordinator when I got to Tech was Charley Pell, who later went on to become the head coach at Clemson and Florida. He's the best coach I have ever been around. ... He was very organized and he was a very good communicator and an excellent

Notes on Rick Razzano

Name:	Richard Anthony Razzano
Born:	November 15, 1955
Hometown:	New Castle, Pennsylvania
Current residence:	Milford, Ohio
Occupation:	Retired. After a seven-year pro football career, Razzano ran his own business for 16 years. He was in the wholesale ice cream distribution business.
Position:	Middle linebacker
Height/Playing weight:	5-11, 225
Years lettered:	1974-77
Accomplishments:	Razzano dominates the tackling statistics page in the Tech record book. He led the Hokies in tackles all four years, and his 177 stops in 1975 are a record he shares with Scott Hill, who did it in 1987. Razzano also has the single-game record of 30 tackles and the career record of 634 tackles. He had 21 unassisted tackles in a 1975 game against Richmond. Razzano was inducted into the Tech Sports Hall of Fame in 1997, the same year as current Tech coach Frank Beamer.
The game:	Virginia Tech at Auburn, October 4, 1975

motivator. He was a no-nonsense guy, full of piss and vinegar. All of us believed in him in a big way."

The Sharpe-Razzano era did not start off well. The team lost its first four games. It then fell behind South Carolina 17-0 on the road in the fifth.

"We go running off the field and the entire corner of the end zone was ridiculing our squad," Razzano remembers. "They were all yelling, 'Gobble, gobble, gobble.' Well, we really got upset with that. We came out and kicked off and our backup fullback, Tony Houff, went down and just cracked this kid. I think everybody in the stands heard it. He just waylaid this kid. That got us excited. We went on and shut them out in the second half and scored 31 points.

"We went on and won four games that season, not bad with a new staff, a new system, and a bunch of new players."

Expectations were high for the next season after the solid finish in 1974. They were dimmed somewhat by the 1-2 start. The Hokies expected a lot out of themselves, but opened the year with losses at Kentucky and at Kent State. Tech won at home against Richmond in its third game, but was back on the road again the following week, at Auburn. With games against Florida State and Virginia coming up, a loss against Auburn would have put the team in a tenuous position. It needed to win badly at a place where it was—and still is—difficult to win if you're wearing enemy colors.

Game Results

Behind the running of Roscoe Coles and Phil Rogers, Tech put together a strong offensive game against Auburn. Both players rushed for over 100 yards in the game, and greatly helped the Hokies to a 23-16 lead late in the game.

Auburn had a final chance. With 4:06 to play, it took over on its own 20. Over the next two and a half minutes, the Tigers pounded the ball up the field, advancing to the Tech 5-yard line with 1:25 on the clock.

There isn't a linebacker alive who doesn't love a chance at a goal-line stand, and Razzano was no different. He and his mates knew the stakes: Keep the Tigers out of the end zone and the Hokies would win. The first 75 yards of the drive came too easily. It was time to toughen up. Razzano and his teammates were determined. The Tigers weren't getting into the end zone.

Joe Namath had an indirect hand in helping Virginia Tech recruit Rick Razzano.

Auburn tried to run in the middle of the line on the first play, right at Razzano, who stuffed the runner for no gain. Teammate Bill Houseright did the honors on second down, also for no gain. Defensive pressure led to an incomplete pass on third down, and then Razzano, Houseright, and others forced Auburn quarterback Clyde Baumgartner out of bounds four yards short of the end zone. Tech got the ball back with 28 seconds left and kneeled down for the victory.

"I'm shaking all over," Sharpe said in his postgame comments. "That was the greatest display of guts and sportsmanship I've ever been associated with. I guess we screwed up the fearless forecasters."

Razzano calls it "maybe the greatest stand in Virginia Tech history. I guarantee you it was the stand of the century. It was a great victory, to beat Auburn. It was a tremendous accomplishment for a team that at the time no one had really heard about.

"Every goal-line stand is huge. They're definitely difference-makers for every player, every team. If you hold them to three points, you win. If you hold them to none, you really win.

"They got all the way to the five and we stopped them. I remember that feeling, it's just elation. You feel so good for the entire squad and for the university, for all the players past and present. It is a huge moment in history when you stop a team like Auburn first and goal at the five. It was awesome.

"That absolutely was a turning point of the season."

Tech only lost once more the rest of the way, a three-point defeat at West Virginia. The team closed with four straight victories to finish 8-3. That season was the high point of Sharpe's career and Razzano's personal best.

"We had a great season my sophomore year," recalls Razzano. "We were a tremendous team. Our offense was rolling. Phil Rogers was moved from tailback to quarterback. What he was able to do with his wheels was incredible. Defensively we were stout.

"The last game of the season, we were facing Wake Forest. Coach Sharpe told us that the Tangerine Bowl officials had already informed him if we beat Wake Forest we were going to be in that bowl game. We went out and beat them 40-10. Unfortunately, in the next day or two they decided to take South Carolina and Miami of Ohio. It's our contention that we would

Razzano (38) does his part in a crucial goal-line stand in the fourth quarter at Auburn.

have gone out in the morning and beaten South Carolina, and then beaten Miami at night. That's how good we were.

"Then we went to Christmas break and ... when we came back [we learned that] Coach Pell had taken the job at Clemson. The team was really, really upset and disappointed. He was the guy on defense."

In 1976, Tech started 6-2 before losing three straight to close the season. Then came Razzano's senior season of 1977, a year he calls "a catastrophe." A teammate, Bob Vorhies, died in November after being required to run punishment drills. The school settled a lawsuit filed by Vorhies' family four years later. The team went 3-7-1 on the field and had to win its final two games to get to that record. The day after the season ended, Sharpe was fired.

"It was not a good thing for our squad," Razzano says. "It turned out good because they hired Coach [Bill] Dooley and he took us to the next level, and then they hired Coach [Frank] Beamer.

"It was a lot of traumatic stuff for a bunch of 18-, 19-, 20-year-old kids to go through."

Reflecting on Tech

Several of Razzano's teammates had sons who went on to play for Tech. Houseright was one, Tom Beasley was another. Razzano thought for a while that he was going to join that club. His eldest son, Rick Jr., went to Mississippi before going on to the NFL. His middle son Joey signed with Tech only to be denied admission because he was lacking one science class. He ended up going to the University of Kentucky.

It's a situation that still bothers Razzano, though he concedes everything worked out for everyone involved.

"I've never talked to Coach Beamer about it. To me, that's what really disappoints me," he says. "I never understood why they did that, why they recruited [Joey] so hard, offered him so early, and then a couple days prior to the national signing date called and said, 'By the way, we want Joey to take chemistry in the summer. His sophomore science doesn't meet our standards.' He ended up signing because I felt I could work it out, which I tried to do.

"He's moved on, they've moved on, we've moved on. Things work out for the best. I just never did understand how veteran coaches could let that slip by."

The situation didn't sour his feelings for Virginia Tech, the school that gave the undersized linebacker his chance.

"I owe them," Razzano says. "I couldn't have written a better script as far as the enjoyment I got out of [my time there] and the contacts that I made and the friendships, the relationships that were made. The neat thing about most sporting teams is that locker room and those dorms, it's those times you'll never forget regardless of how long you're away from somebody. When you get back together, it's like you never left.

"I have nothing but fond memories of Virginia Tech."

CHAPTER 9

CYRUS LAWRENCE

Virginia Tech and Cyrus Lawrence may have been the perfect fit. Lawrence was a workhorse at Southampton High under legendary coach Wayne Cosby. During Lawrence's senior season at Southampton, Bill Dooley took over as Tech's coach after a successful run at the University of North Carolina. And "run" it was—Dooley was famous for loving the running game and the "three yards and a cloud of dust" style.

He wanted a back to carry the ball a lot, and he found his man in Lawrence.

"He believed in running backs, especially tailbacks, and that was my game," Lawrence says. "I believed in their program, believed they were building a good one for the future."

Lawrence wasn't very big, and he wasn't a speed burner. He was a power back—exceptionally strong and hard to bring down.

"He had great vision," Tech's running backs coach Billy Hite says. "For 10 yards, he was as fast as anybody on the field. He had a great stance and a great start. He could come out of his stance like no one I'd ever seen."

Lawrence says he arrived at Tech well prepared: "Coach Cosby taught me a lot of things that I was able to take with me to Tech. I worked hard in the offseason and I was up to the chore. I was ready. Every back is different, has his forte. Mine was inside running, tough running, running over you, through you, whatever it takes. I did it.

"The offenses we used at my high school and at Tech were similar, [as was] how we were trained. I always enjoyed running the ball. That was my strength. As the game went on, I got stronger. Ten or 15 carries didn't do it for me. I was just warming up."

On Lawrence's second carry as a Hokie, he went 59 yards for a touchdown. That was his longest run at Tech, and it was a rarity. He only had 14 runs that covered 20 or more yards in his career, and only three that went more than 40 yards.

Lawrence did it in bulk.

The Setting

The 1981 season started with such promise. The Hokies were coming off a season in which they won eight games and played in the Peach Bowl. It was their first winning season in three years under coach Bill Dooley. They followed that up by opening 4-0 in 1981. The season was bright with promise—or, so it seemed. The next six games brought four losses. Particularly dispiriting was the last of those. On a bitterly cold, windy, snowy day at Lane Stadium, Virginia Military Institute came in and beat Tech 6-0. That came a week after Tech lost by seven at Miami.

"We should have won both of those games," says Lawrence.

One game remained. The Hokies had to travel to Charlottesville to play their archrival, the University of Virginia Cavaliers. Losing five of their final seven and their last three would be no way to end the season. They had to have this one.

"We made a pledge that we had to go out and play our best. Mentally, we were ready," Lawrence recalls.

Tech's tailback rushed for 1,221 yards as a sophomore to set a school record. Now, in his junior year, he remained just 21 yards from breaking his own record. He saved his best for the last game of the season.

Game Results

The Hokies started their late-November game against the Cavaliers doing what they often did: handing the ball to Lawrence. The tailback carried the ball, and carried the ball, again and again and again. Lawrence had 16 games during his career in which he surpassed the 100-yard mark in a game. But he had just one where he topped 200: against the Cavaliers to

Notes on Cyrus Lawrence

Name:	Cyrus Christopher Lawrence
Born:	November 15, 1960
Hometown:	Franklin, Virginia
Current residence:	Franklin, Virginia
Occupation:	Lawrence is a marketing representative for Lorillard Tobacco of Greensboro, North Carolina, a job he's had for 18 years.
Position:	Tailback
Height/Playing weight:	5-9, 203
Years lettered:	1979-82
Accomplishments:	Lawrence led Tech in rushing each of his first three seasons, going over the 1,000-yard mark as a sophomore and junior. His 3,767 career yards remain the all-time high. He also holds records with 42 rushes in one game, 325 rushes in one season, and 843 rushes for a career. Lawrence had 16 games with at least 100 yards, the most of any back in Tech history. He is a member of the Tech Athletic Hall of Fame.
The game:	Virginia Tech at Virginia, November 28, 1981

close his junior season. Lawrence rushed 38 times for 202 yards as the Hokies closed the season with a 20-3 victory.

"Cyrus Lawrence is definitely one of the best runners in college football," Dooley said after the game. "He showed it out there today. You can't arm-tackle Cyrus and he has amazing balance. I wouldn't swap him for any back anywhere."

Lawrence even caught two passes that day, half of his career total.

"Cyrus did a lot of things well," Hite says, "but he didn't have the greatest hands in the world."

Lawrence chuckles at that memory before defending his pass-catching ability.

"We didn't throw a lot to the running backs in high school and Tech was pretty much the same," he says. "We were going to line up and we were going to run it down your throat. I always considered myself to have good hands. I could catch the football. I was never given that opportunity in games; it's just the way the scheme went. It's a bridge we never really crossed."

That Virginia game, he says, was the best of many outstanding days he had in a Tech uniform. Going over the 200-yard mark made it special. Ending the season on a good note made it special. Beating Virginia made it special.

"We'd come off losing those two games, very critical games actually that would have set us up for another bowl game if we had made a better appearance," Lawrence remembers. "The Virginia game is always a highlight and it gets you really, really pumped up anyway. It's one of those things you cannot put into words. ... We were very psyched for the game.

"Coach Dooley set is in a good mental stage in the middle of the week. [Our coaches] never really got frustrated with us. We should have won those games but they never lost faith in us as a team, and that really stuck with us. Of course, there were a lot of write-ups during the week and some things Virginia may have said against us stoked the fire a little higher. We believed in ourselves. Our record did not indicate the ballclub we had. We had a good team."

Lawrence feels the win over the Cavaliers was the biggest win that season for the Hokies.

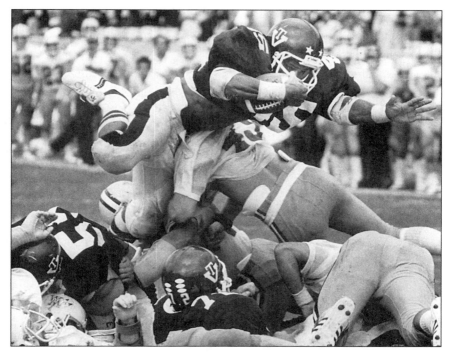

Cyrus Lawrence was a workhorse back at Virginia Tech with 843 career carries.

"Winning a state rivalry, in style, kind of erased a lot of things about how we played previously," Lawrence says. "You always want to end on a strong note. My contributions to that game were good. I had a lot of help as always. It's not a one-man game. If that tackle doesn't make that block or that guard doesn't make that block, Cyrus doesn't run anywhere. I had faith in them, they had faith in me. As a unit, we knew what we had to do as a team, and we did it.

"It was my type of game. I'd had some big games before, lots of yards. But having a 200-yard game against a state rival was my most outstanding."

* * *

For the past 20-plus years, Hite has tried to have two backs he can call "No. 1." His reason for that is simple: He's convinced he ran Lawrence too much. Hite can recall in vivid detail watching Lawrence injure his left knee in a practice session, costing him most of his senior year and a chance at a professional career. The fact that Lawrence doesn't blame too much running for his injury still doesn't sway Hite.

"He plants and cuts and bang, his ACL just exploded," Hite recalls. "He never got touched. Here we've lost him for the year and when he went to the NFL combine, he flunks the physical because of his knee. That kept him from having a shot in the NFL. From that point on, I said I'd never play one guy again and just run him to death. That's when my philosophy changed.

"When you get hit that many times, something is bound to happen eventually. Just how freak it was without getting hit … that's when I started thinking, he's been hit so many times, and he didn't need to get hit for that to happen."

Lawrence did run it a lot. His records of 325 carries in one season and 843 for a career aren't likely to be broken, but Lawrence isn't ruling out that possibility.

"Sooner or later, someone is going to get my career rushing mark," he says. "Records are meant to be broken. Kevin Jones broke my single-season record, and there are others that may have been broken that I don't even know about yet.

"I've never been a records guy—that wasn't my goal. Every game was a challenge. Whatever came out of that was from working hard, from it being a team effort. Records are something that you don't really set out to do. Those things happen through hard work, not just by yourself but from a lot of others, too."

He wonders sometimes what might have happened if he hadn't injured that knee. Surely he would have cracked the 4,000-yard mark for his career. He only missed by 233 yards. He may have even had a pro career.

But he blames no one. Running the ball is what he did, and he wanted to do it a lot. Injuries are a part of the game, and there was no reason one couldn't happen to him.

"I had damaged the knee in a game earlier that year—that's what started it. The ACL was weakened," he says. "The knee is a funny thing. The doctors told me my legs were strong, and that helped cover some of the damage that was in the knee.

"You have to take life as it comes. I never blamed anybody because that's part of the ballgame. I never look back at that."

Lawrence's only 200-yard day came his junior season against arch-rival Virginia.

Reflecting on Tech

Lawrence always believed in playing every game like it was his last. It's a lesson he imparts on his three sons now: Do everything you do as well as it can be done because nothing is guaranteed beyond the moment.

"I had a good career, made a lot of good friends and got a good education," Lawrence concludes. "You have to look at it in a three-

67

dimensional way. You're only going to play so many years. Something can happen. I'm a prime example. I had my education to fall back on.

"I never look back on anything as being unfinished. Every game, I always gave 120 percent. ... I always knew in my heart that when my time came and someone asked, 'Could you have played better?' I'd be able to say no. I knew that every game I did play, I did my best. That's all anybody can ask."

CHAPTER 10

BRUCE SMITH

Football wasn't the only thing Bruce Smith did not take for granted. Tops on that list are his parents, the late George W. Smith and his mother Annie Lee Smith. They were not a family of means. Smith's parents gave everything they had in order to provide for their children.

"It started back when I was growing up," Smith says of the work ethic that carried him to the top of his profession. "My parents made sacrifices to make sure I would have an opportunity to be in the position I was in. They always wanted something better for all their children than they had in the way of opportunities. I had seen some of the struggles they went through, how they were treated. I had seen segregation to a certain degree. They wanted me to be able to enjoy life with my family and not have to work as hard as they did.

"My dad would wake up at 6 a.m. and sometimes not get in until six in the evening. Then my father would find the strength and energy to take me to whatever practice I had at the time—baseball, basketball, football. I often look back on those experiences and wonder how they were able to do it. That kept me going.

"If they could make those sacrifices and keep doing the things that they were not enjoying, then what I could accomplish was endless. I loved what I was doing."

Smith excelled on the football field, but he was a pretty fair basketball player, too. Imagine trying to go up and get a rebound away from him. "I'd put my hip on somebody," he says with a laugh. He had scholarship offers in the sport and even had a chance to play it while at Virginia Tech. He declined because he thought that trying to play both sports and keep up with his schoolwork would spread him too thin. Besides, football was his first love.

"Football chose me, I didn't choose football," he says. "Just being the biggest kid—I was 6 feet, 3 inches, 270 pounds in high school."

Tech coach Bill Dooley had an idea he was getting a ferocious player when he signed Smith out of Booker T. Washington High in Norfolk, Virginia.

"We started recruiting Bruce early," Dooley says. "All of a sudden, everybody in the country—everybody, I don't care who it was—got involved.

"Bruce was an unbelievable athlete. He had the footwork of a defensive back and the strength of a defensive lineman. He had an unbelievable attitude on the field to do his best. Everybody started double-teaming him. We'd have him at nose guard one time, had him at defensive tackle the next, at end the next. They couldn't get enough blocking schemes to stop him.

"He was an intimidating player. Offensively they knew they had to account for him, had to take care of him or they weren't going to get the ball off. He had the ability to run down backs if they'd try and sweep away from him."

Simply put, Bruce Smith was a beast. And he was going to Tech.

The Setting

Smith had exceptional talent and a work ethic to match. It was a combination that made him one of the nation's best football players, let alone one of the best to ever wear a Virginia Tech uniform. He hardly needed any additional ammunition when he stepped on the field, but he had it anyway. A back injury cut short his sophomore season and caused Smith to do plenty of thinking. He realized he could take nothing for granted. One snap and it could all be over.

"I was coming off an injury where I slightly crushed a vertebrae," Smith recalls. "I was out the rest of the year, and something just went off in my head academically and athletically that this can be taken away from me at any point in time.

Notes on Bruce Smith

Name:	Bruce B. Smith
Born:	June 18, 1963
Hometown:	Norfolk, Virginia
Current residence:	Virginia Beach, Virginia
Occupation:	Smith has founded Bruce Smith Enterprises, a development company that deals with a variety of real estate projects.
Position:	Defensive Tackle
Height/Playing weight:	6-3, 273
Years lettered:	1981-84
Accomplishments:	Smith's list of accomplishments could fill a book on their own. He was the 1984 Outland trophy winner as the top lineman in the country, and was a consensus All-American that year. He was an All-American as a junior, too. He had four sacks in a game (twice), 22 sacks in a season, and 46 for his career—all records. He had 31 tackles for loss in a season and 71 for a career, both records. The losses totaled more than 500 yards. Smith was the No. 1 pick in the 1985 draft and he finished a 19-year pro career as the NFL's all-time sack leader with 199.
The game:	Duke at Virginia Tech, October 8, 1983

"I just decided I was going to play every game I could possibly play to the fullest. Things just started clicking."

Did they ever. As a junior, Smith set records with 22 sacks and 31 total tackles behind the line of scrimmage. People were noticing the defensive tackle. Those who didn't got an eyeful when Duke, led by talented quarterback and future professional Ben Bennett, came to Lane Stadium for the fifth game of the year in 1983.

Game Results

Duke got through the first quarter of its matchup with Virginia Tech without having to sweat too much. But the second quarter was much different. Early in the period, Smith got in his stance and locked eyes on Bennett. Even when he wasn't making tackles, Smith messed up an opponents' offense because it took several people to block him—or try to block him. Even that wasn't enough a lot of the time.

Bennett knows he became a Smith fan the day the Blue Devils played in Lane Stadium. Now a coach in the Arena Football League, Bennett saw way too much of Smith in one afternoon.

"No one had ever heard of Bruce at that point. They had after that game," Bennett says. "I take a lot of credit for that. His coming out was against me. That game spurred him on to his professional heights. I should probably get a 10-percent cut."

Later as professionals, Bennett got to know Smith. Like anyone else who has dealt with him, he came away impressed.

"He's always very pleasant and polite, a heck of a guy," Bennett says.

On the field was another story. With each snap of the ball, Smith exploded off the line, a "trained killer," Bennett says. By the time Duke made it out of Blacksburg that day, Smith had sacked Bennett four times. Three of those came in the second quarter. The total loss was 35 yards. Duke finished the day with minus-four rushing yards. Its first seven drives ended with a punt. Then Bennett threw an interception. Then came two more punts. Tech ended up winning 27-14.

"I remember that [game] very well," says Smith. "Ben and I got to become very good friends during that game. ... I was having a hell of a lot of fun.

As a junior, Bruce Smith sacked Duke's Ben Bennett four times.

"When you're having fun, no matter what you do in life, that's when you are going to be the most successful. Doesn't matter if you are a doctor, lawyer, construction worker, or athlete. If you truly enjoy [your job], you will do well. That's what happened in my case, particularly on that day."

It wasn't as much fun on the other side.

"That would be an understatement," Bennett says. "We put two linemen on him. We put a guard and a fullback, even a couple of cheerleaders. No one could stop him. He actually knocked me out twice in the same game. He knocked me out once, and knocked me stupid another time.

"The first couple of sacks, he was pretty juiced, and I was a little pissed. The next 13-14 times he hit me, the enthusiasm for the project had waned a little bit and I wasn't so pissed. When he knocked me silly at the end of the game, my mind said, 'Get up and go back to the huddle.' My legs said, 'We'll have none of that.' Someone caught me and said, 'Wait for your trainer.' I didn't realize until after I watched the tape that it was Smith who helped me up."

Reflecting on Tech

Smith's final two years were as good as any defensive lineman had enjoyed up to that point. When he left Tech, he had a long professional career that ended with him atop the NFL's all-time sacks list. He was 40 years old when he stopped, and he never really slowed down.

"You're a better man than I am [if you were able to predict that kind of success coming out of high school]," Smith says. "I didn't foresee it. It was a blessing the way my career turned out.

"There are breaks that are made along the way, whether it is in academics, sports, or what have you. There's a break that comes along in people's lives and they have to recognize that break. My break was athletics.

"Had it not been for my athletics, I would not have received a scholarship. Who knows what path I would have traveled? Certainly each and every individual has a talent that's within them. It's up to that individual to go out and explore and try different things in life and find out what that talent is and get it developed.

Smith is one of the most decorated players ever to wear a **Virginia Tech** uniform.

"I can't say if I'd be where I am today without my athletic career. I would say I would have been at a disadvantage. I know I would not have been afforded the same opportunities I had when I was coming out of college. Certainly these kinds of opportunities don't come a person's way in the everyday walk of life.

"Don't get me wrong. I worked my ass off to put myself in this position. But athletics definitely helped create some opportunities for me."

Smith has stayed involved with the school, spending time on the Tech Board of Visitors. It was an appropriate position, since he and his family are frequent visitors, for both football and basketball games.

"It is a joy to be able to take my son back and let him see where my wife and I attended school," Smith says. "I wouldn't say it all began for me there, but it was certainly a major point in my life and my career, and I cherish the time I spent at Tech."

CHAPTER 11

JIM PYNE

While he was playing football at Virginia Tech, Jim Pyne learned something that both amazed and thrilled him. His father, George Pyne III, had played in the National Football League. He was a defensive lineman for the Boston Patriots. Pyne's grandfather, George Pyne Jr., had also played in the NFL. He was a two-way lineman for the old Providence Steamrollers, who later became the Chicago Bears. If young Pyne made an NFL roster, the family would become the first three-generation family in NFL history.

"To be the first to ever do anything is a great honor," Pyne says. "I met my grandfather when I was 2-to-3 years old. I really don't remember him. What I know of him is as an athlete. To see his old leather helmets, to hear about him, to hear around town that he was a great player is cool. I got a couple of letters a few years ago from a guy who had played with him and he told me all kinds of things about him.

"To do what he did, to do what my dad did ... these guys were my heroes growing up. Family is everything and that little niche in history we have is a very nice thing."

Pyne did end up playing nine years in the NFL but first his path took him to Blacksburg and Tech. He ended up being one of the key players in the resurgence of the Virginia Tech program.

The path that led Pyne to Tech is as interesting as the path that eventually led him from Tech to the NFL. Pyne's father didn't let him play football until Pyne was in the seventh grade. All his buddies started playing much earlier and were much more advanced when Pyne finally showed up to play.

"I didn't really know what all to do, and they were kind of laughing at me," Pyne says.

His "rookie" initiation? Pyne was told to get down in a stance and go one-on-one with another player. The other player happened to be the son of the team's coach. Pyne did as he was told.

"I got down in the stance and closed my eyes," he recalls with a laugh. "When I looked up afterward, the kid was on the ground. I liked that."

A star was born. Pyne quickly showed he had the same knack for the game that his father and grandfather had. When it came time to pick a college, a lot of schools were clamoring to be the choice. At this point, another George Pyne got involved. Pyne's older brother, George Pyne IV, played collegiately at Brown University. Two of his former coaches there, Denny Marie and Tommy Groome, had since moved to Tech. They placed a phone call to Pyne's brother and asked him, "How do we get your brother?"

"He told them, tongue in cheek, 'Get your head coach on an airplane and get him up here and you'll probably get him,' says Pyne.

Tech coach Frank Beamer got on a plane and got up there. And sure enough, he got Pyne.

"I really liked [Coach Beamer], and when I got down there and saw the school, I really liked the place and the people. It was just a fit," Pyne says.

The Setting

It turned out to be an excellent fit. Despite a strong New England accent that wasn't heard much around those parts, Pyne fit in perfectly at the school and in the small town. He was a starter by the time his true freshman season was half over.

"Jim Pyne was one of the toughest guys ever," says Bill Roth, the team's long-time broadcaster. "He looked good with mud on his face and grass in his helmet. Fundamentally, he was just a great center."

To understand the importance of the Syracuse game in 1993 or any game that season, it's important to first look back a bit. The 1993 season was Beamer's mulligan. It had to be straight down the middle. These days, Beamer has a contract that pays him $2 million a year. He's one of the most

Notes on Jim Pyne

Name:	James M. Pyne
Born:	November 23, 1971
Hometown:	Milford, Massachusetts
Current residence:	Tampa, Florida
Occupation:	Pyne coached in the National Football League for three years after his nine-year playing career ended, and is now exploring private business opportunities in Florida.
Position:	Center
Height/Playing weight:	6-3, 285
Years lettered:	1990-93
Accomplishments:	Pyne became Virginia Tech's first unanimous All-America selection in 1993. That year, Tech averaged 444.1 yards and 36.4 points per game. He became a starter during his true freshman season and ended up playing more than 2,700 snaps. The man he was responsible for blocking recorded only one sack. He earned the Dudley Award as the state of Virginia's player of the year in 1993. Pyne's number 73 has been retired, he is in the school's Hall of Fame, and the offensive line meeting room is named after him.
The game:	Syracuse at Virginia Tech, November 13, 1993

respected coaches in the game. But he, like many other coaches, faced a be-good-or-be-gone year, and 1993 was that year.

Pyne's freshman year of 1990 was Beamer's fourth and the team produced its second straight winning season by going 6-5. After the season, Beamer had a chance to jump to Boston College. He turned down the job and stuck with his alma mater. Tech slipped to 5-6 in 1991. Then came the total disaster of 1992. The Hokies finished 2-8-1, bad enough all by itself. Four of the losses and the tie came in games that Tech led in the fourth quarter. The worst was a game at Rutgers on Halloween. Tech jumped out to a 35-6 lead. Rutgers won 50-49. Rutgers had to go 65 yards in 14 seconds with no timeouts to win the game, and did. Lots and lots of people wanted Beamer's head, a fact the players knew well.

"Things were falling apart," Pyne recalls. "The players are trained to say the right things and not talk about it, but we all knew and we all talked about it, more than you might think.

"We knew the program was on the fence. We had all come in with Coach Beamer and his staff, we liked all those guys. Who knows what might have happened if they'd fired Coach Beamer!"

Dave Braine, the school's athletic director at the time, never really gave that much thought, as it turned out. He stuck with Beamer for a variety of reasons. Beamer was loyal to the school and took over at a time when it was on probation. Beamer had the pieces in place for success. Beamer was a good coach who had a bad year. Braine suggested some changes may be in order and Beamer did end up replacing three assistants.

"A great call when a lot of people were saying fire him," Pyne said. "He saw Coach Beamer was a good guy who *is* Virginia Tech. He went there. We had the talent. We knew we were close."

Everyone knew 1993 was huge.

"We knew we could be pretty good, we didn't know quite how good," Pyne said. "We just knew we had to win some games."

The Hokies did that. They won six of their first nine, scoring a lot of points along the way. They had 63 against Pittsburgh, 55 against Maryland, 55 against Temple and 49 again against Rutgers—this time that was good enough for a victory. Maurice DeShazo was settling into a groove at quarterback after a rough 1992. And he was protected by a great line led by Pyne.

Jim Pyne followed his father and grandfather into the NFL, making the Pynes the league's first three-generation family.

The Syracuse game, the tenth of the season, loomed huge. The Hokies were coming off a loss at Boston College. They were still in the hunt for a bowl slot, which would be their first under Beamer. Talk was they'd get a bid after the Syracuse game—if they won.

Game Results

To beat Syracuse, Pyne knew he'd have to have an excellent day against a guy, Syracuse nose guard Kevin Mitchell, who didn't allow many offensive linemen to have those kinds of days against him. Mitchell was one of the nation's best defensive players, and would end up the season as the most valuable defensive player in the Fiesta Bowl. He made the all-Big East Conference team twice, and went on to play nine years in the National Football League.

"Kevin was strong, tough and quick—he was a linebacker playing nose guard," Pyne says. "I never saw anybody block him."

A tad undersized, Pyne had been dealing with an underdog's mentality all his life. The "he can't do it" challenges were what drove him, and proving himself against the likes of Mitchell was important to him.

That season, Bryan Stinespring, who is now Tech's offensive coordinator, was in his first year as a full-time assistant coach. Helping with the offensive line was one of his responsibilities. He knew how big the Pyne-Mitchell matchup would be.

"We had a marquee offensive lineman in Jim Pyne and they had a marquee defensive lineman in Kevin Mitchell," Stinespring says. "Kevin was a tough player who could singlehandedly wreak havoc on a team. It was two great players who ended up waging a war of wills.

"Our ability to be able to run the ball against the underfront they played was going to be very critical to us winning the ballgame."

Tech not only won, it won big. It led 21-0 after the first quarter and ended up winning 45-24. The Hokies rushed for 246 yards and three touchdowns. They ran the ball for 185 yards in the second half. Mitchell didn't have a bad day, finishing with 10 tackles. But only one of his tackles was behind the line of scrimmage, and it resulted in just one lost yard. No other Syracuse lineman recorded a sack that day, either.

During his four years at Tech, the man Pyne was responsible for blocking only recorded one sack.

"There's no question—I had many great moments there but that game was the highlight," Pyne says. "We pounded the heck out of the them running the ball. It was fun."

After the game, DeShazo told the *Richmond Times-Dispatch* that Mitchell "is every bit as good as they say. But I spent most of the day just kind of watching Jim go after him. Believe me, the boy is an All-American."

Calvert Jones, a former Tech player who was working in the school's football office that year, told the newspaper that Pyne "was taking Mitchell on what we call the Pyne Ride. He'd just take him right off the ball and drive him 15, 20 yards downfield. He dominated him."

Will Stewart, the managing editor of the Web site TechSideline.Com, watched the 1993 game against Syracuse with his father.

"Late in the game, when the outcome had been sealed, my father and I decided to watch Pyne, and what we saw was a clinic," Stewart recalls. "Time and time again, Pyne would come out of his stance, get his hands up under the opposition's shoulder pad and drive him 10-15 yards downfield. He spent the fourth quarter just destroying Syracuse's interior defense by himself."

Pyne recalls: "I've always put pressure on myself to do well. I knew before the season that it was going to be one of the biggest games of the year for me. This was one of the games the pros were going to look at, to see how I could do against that kind of competition. I knew I had to do well for me personally and for the team.

"It went well for us because we were able to run the ball. I don't want to brag about how I did. We ran the ball well and I had a good game. It was a fun game, my last game at Lane Stadium. I remember coming out for pregame. People on the high side of the stadium had a big fluorescent green sign that said 'Pyne.' It was really nice and meant a lot to me.

"We went out there and ran the heck out of the ball. The expectations I put on myself, I was able to reach them. It was an awesome feeling."

The best news for Tech came after the game. The Independence Bowl extended the Hokies a bid. They perhaps could have held out a week to see how they'd do against arch-rival Virginia, maybe moved up a bit in the bowl pecking order. That was a risk, however, and for a program that didn't have a single player who had ever been in a bowl, a bid in hand was too good to pass up.

"That we were able to get to a bowl game meant everything to us," Pyne says.

* * *

Tech ended up beating Virginia and then Indiana in the Independence Bowl to finish the 1993 season with a 9-3 record. The Hokies haven't had a season since that didn't end in a bowl trip. They go into the 2006 season with a streak of 13 straight bowl appearances.

It all started Pyne's senior year, and who knows what would have happened had the Hokies not beaten Syracuse?

"Who knows indeed? I haven't done the math on that one," Pyne says. "I'm just glad we were able to win."

Stinespring, one of a handful who has been around for all 13 of those bowls, doesn't try to understate the importance of that one game and that one season.

"It was a significant game for our program," Stinespring says. "That group laid the groundwork for the attitude that still permeates our program. Be tough, be hard-nosed, find a way to win.

"That was Jim. Driven is a good word to describe him but I don't know if that says it all. Everything he did was geared toward making him the best football player he could be."

Chapter 12

BRYAN STILL

Bryan Still doesn't fit into any of the stereotypes many people seem to have about football players. He's not a gung-ho, rah-rah type. Weightlifting? It wasn't really ever a big thing with him. He was different, not in a bad way and not in a divisive way—but different nonetheless. He didn't hang out much with teammates when they went out on the town. He used to avoid the weekly press luncheons the Virginia Tech sports information department arranged because he wasn't enamored of the food that was served. He finally showed up once after being promised a good ol' cheeseburger for lunch.

"To some teammates, he came off as aloof," says Skip Wood, who covered the Still-era Hokies for the *Richmond Times-Dispatch* before becoming a pro football writer at *USA Today*.

"Shy and totally unassuming would be a better description."

Personality aside, Still could run and catch with the best of them. He fell in love with football the first time he played as a youngster growing up in Richmond, Virginia. As a kid, he told anyone who would listen what he wanted to do when he grew up: he was going to be a football player.

Still drew plenty of attention while playing at Huguenot High School. He was all set to go to the University of Maryland, which was going to the run-and-shoot offense—a receiver's dream. Yet he ended up at Tech, far from a receiver's dream come true. At the time Still went to Tech, the school hadn't had anyone catch as many as 40 passes in a season in 11 years, and had never had anyone catch 50 in a season.

"I was a good prospect, one of the top-rated prospects in Richmond at the time," Still says. "I wasn't like a [top-rated national recruit]. I thought I'd go to Maryland and catch a lot of passes.

"My mother was instrumental in me picking Virginia Tech. They had shown interest in me since my junior year and they wanted me. I agreed with that.

"I always felt like I was at home when I went up there, and I liked Coach [Frank] Beamer. I remember him coming and waiting with my mom in my living room for me to get home [from school]. A lot of things led to me going there, [like] the feeling they liked me a lot."

The Setting

Still's first three years overlapped the career of Antonio Freeman, who went on to play alongside Brett Favre in Green Bay for many years. Freeman left Tech as the school's all-time leading receiver, and stayed there until Ernest Wilford broke his career mark in 2003. Like most good receivers, Freeman had someone on the other side who could relieve some of the pressure. That someone was Still, who had great hands and could make the tough catch.

"For a variety of reasons, he was never truly embraced by his coaches," Wood says of Still. "He was a rail-thin player who steadfastly rejected suggestions for more work in the weight room. This annoyed coaches and especially annoyed strength coach Mike Gentry. Not that Still didn't give it a go, but as a sophomore, when the tip of one of his fingers was severed during a weight-machine mishap [it was re-attached], he decided that was just about enough of that.

"But because of Still's great hands and undeniable penchant for acrobatic catches, Frank more or less sighed and let Bryan be Bryan, although he always believed better weight-room work would have prevented Still's minor but assorted injuries."

Still's senior year was his one chance to be "the man" among the receiving corps. Duane Thomas returned in the backfield, and strong-armed Jim Druckenmiller was ready to take over for Maurice DeShazo at quarterback. Tech felt like it could have a strong season in 1995. Then it lost its opener at home to Boston College. Still suffered a shoulder injury and had

Notes on Bryan Still

Name:	Bryan A. Still
Born:	June 3, 1974
Hometown:	Richmond, Virginia
Current residence:	Richmond, Virginia
Occupation:	Still played in the NFL for four seasons and is now a high school health and physical education teacher in Chesterfield County, Virginia. He also plays arena football with the Richmond Bandits of the AIFL.
Position:	Receiver
Height/Playing weight:	6-0, 175
Years lettered:	1992-95
Accomplishments:	Still played alongside Antonio Freeman his first three years at Tech, and thus was the Hokies' second option at receiver. In 1995, he led Tech in receptions for the only time when he caught 32 passes for 628 yards and three touchdowns. Still ranks 13th on the school's all-time list with 74 catches for 1,458 yards and 11 touchdowns. Those totals don't include the 1995 Sugar Bowl, where Still caught six passes for 119 yards and a touchdown. Though he went on to have a pro career, Still never made as much as second-team all-Big East.
The game:	Virginia Tech versus Texas in the Sugar Bowl, December 31, 1995

to sit out the next week. No biggie, it was only Cincinnati coming to Lane Stadium. But Tech lost that one, too, 16-0. Now it was 0-2 and facing a home game against Miami.

"That was a bad loss to Cincinnati. It was like going back to my freshman year, when we went 2-8-1, and that was real bad," Still says. "We had some real good character guys on that 1995 team, guys who were very team oriented and all-around good guys. We just looked at each other and said, 'Let's go, we have to win this game.' And it was a big game coming up.

"Had we lost to Miami like everybody thought we would, that definitely would have been a deep hole we couldn't have climbed out of."

Tech managed to beat Miami 13-7. The team really hit its stride after that game. It won all eight of its remaining games and scored 31 or more points in five of them. A Hokies squad that started 0-2 finished 9-2, earning a spot in the Sugar Bowl opposite Texas.

It was a weird week leading up to the bowl game. One of the bigger story lines concerned a Texas player who was an "imposter." He had played some college football years earlier under his real name and now was trying to play again under a fake name. There was also a sense that Tech didn't belong on such a stage with a "name" program like Texas. The "Who are these guys?" theme got quite a workout in newspapers that week.

"I can't say I ever sensed disrespect. I can't remember anyone saying anything negative about us," Still says. "But I did definitely feel a lot of that 'Who are these guys?' stuff, no question. We put together good years the previous two and had been to bowls. We were 9-2. I can understand that people might be wondering what a Virginia Tech was doing going to the Sugar Bowl.

"We knew Texas had a big name and a good team. They had Ricky Williams and Shon Mitchell running the ball, James Brown at quarterback. People were talking about the 'BMW backfield.' We had just started winning some games and this was the first really big bowl for that group of guys. The previous year we had played Tennessee in the Gator Bowl and we got blown out [45-23]. We wanted to make up for that, and prove we belonged."

The night before the game, Still had a dream. Not only did the Hokies win against Texas in his dream, Still also became the game's Most Valuable Player.

Bryan Still had a lot to celebrate during Virginia Tech's victory over Texas in the Sugar Bowl.

"A long time ago, somebody told me if you think it and dream it, it will come true," Still says. "I spent a lot of time that whole week just thinking about it being my last college game, looking forward to doing big things so I could move on and try to play in the [NFL].

"The night before the game, I tried to think good things, positive things, how good a game I was going to have, just seeing myself doing good things. I definitely dreamed we would win, and that I would do good things, be the hero of the game."

Game Results

Bryan Still stood by himself on the artificial turf of the Louisiana Superdome, waiting to field a punt as the first half wound down in Virginia Tech's Sugar Bowl meeting with Texas. A million thoughts flooded his brain.

He didn't usually return punts for the Hokies. After a shoulder injury earlier in the season, Tech coach Frank Beamer wanted Still to concentrate on his receiving duties and not risk further injury by fielding punts and taking more hits.

But the Hokies were in trouble against Texas—down 10-0 with less than three minutes remaining in the first half—and Beamer desperately wanted to change his team's fortunes. When the Tech defense held the Longhorns deep in their own territory, Beamer turned to Still for the punt return. His message was simple: Make something happen.

Still trotted out and told himself to make sure of one thing—catch the ball before you do anything else. He wasn't thinking touchdown. He was thinking that he needed a good return to give Tech a chance to get some points before halftime. Beamer had called for a middle return, which is as simple as it sounds. Still tucked the ball in safely and started running straight ahead. He got about five yards before a Texas defender had him within reach. Still sidestepped him and quickly sensed that this was a return that could do more than put Tech in a good position to score.

Before he had time to think, Still realized he was sailing down the sideline, the end zone in sight. Seconds later, Tech was on the board thanks to Still's 60-yard touchdown return.

"It all happened so quick," Still recalls. "The ball was kicked, I caught it, and the next thing I knew I was running up the sidelines.

"When I got by that first guy from Texas, I thought, 'Man, I got it now.' I stepped toward the sideline and that was it. I coasted into the end zone and started celebrating with my teammates. On the sidelines, everybody was saying, 'Now we're ready, here we go now.' It was a feeling everybody had. We never felt we were out of the game, and now people felt we had a chance to go ahead and win the game."

After a rough start, the momentum was beginning to swing in Tech's favor.

"The game started out just like our season had—we were down and we came back to win the game," says Still. "As the game was going along, it seemed like Texas was taking control, and it wasn't going our way. We were jumping offsides, taking penalties, not moving the ball on offense. But Texas never really got full control, and we were still in the game.

The Sugar Bowl MVP award in 1995 went to Still, who had dreamed about winning that award.

"My punt return gave us a jump-start, a ray of hope that we could come back. At that point, it seemed like we had taken over the game, and we started playing like we had the previous nine games. We just ran from there. Jim Druckenmiller had a great game at quarterback, and a lot of guys on our defense played well.

"We didn't have a star player or a guy who stood out as our No. 1 go-to guy. That Sugar Bowl was the last time a lot of us were together so we wanted to get down there and let it all hang out."

The scored remained 10-7 for most of the third quarter. At almost the exact time on the clock as his second-quarter punt return, Still caught a 27-yard pass from Druckenmiller on Texas' 2-yard line. From there, Marcus Parker scored the touchdown that put Tech ahead. Just four minutes later,

Tech broke it open when Still and Druckenmiller connected for a 54-yard touchdown.

"Jim audibled to that," Still says. "He saw Texas in a blitz. When they blitzed, they did it all out with like nine guys and two guys out there covering. We'd been working on that and we'd told Jim if he saw it to try and take advantage and hit a home run. He saw it and was excited, I could see it in his eyes. He gave me the signal to run the post, and I looked up and saw the guy right on me. I didn't see a safety and I thought, shoot, this is going to be wide open. Druck just laid it right out there, and that was the point I knew we were going to win."

Tech added a touchdown later in the fourth quarter, when Jim Baron returned a fumble 20 yards. That made the final score 28-10. Still finished with six catches for 119 yards and one huge punt return.

At the postgame press conference, Still was on the dais right next to Beamer. He was holding the MVP trophy he dreamed about winning the night before.

"In big games, players who have big hearts rise to the occasion," Beamer said in his postgame comments. "We want this guy to touch the ball as many times as he can during the ballgame."

As if his week wasn't big enough, Still got an added bonus. Not long before the game, Beamer told Still he'd been invited to the NFL scouting combine in Indianapolis. Still ended up being drafted in the second round, with the 41st pick overall, by the San Diego Chargers.

"I'd been waiting all year, wondering if I was going to get to go [to the combine]," Still says. "I knew I was going to run fast, jump high, and catch the ball—and if they'd see that, [I'd get to play] in the league. ... I felt like I could play at that level during my junior year. I was a starting receiver on a Division I team that was winning games and going to bowls. I was paired up with a guy like Antonio, and I was learning some things from him."

Life After Tech

Still's pro career didn't work out exactly like he wanted. He played for too many different coaches and coordinators in San Diego. He wasn't terribly happy being so far from home. He tried to catch on with some other NFL teams after he left San Diego, but nothing panned out.

Still got into the end zone on a punt return and on a pass reception in the Sugar Bowl.

Still came home and started his career in teaching. Before long, he was playing flag football for fun, and then he was back in pads playing minor league arena football.

"The travel is terrible, but the games are fun," Still says. "I still love to play the game."

CHAPTER 13

COREY MOORE

Corey Moore was not interviewed for this chapter. He could not be located, despite considerable effort by plenty of people. As much of an enigma as he was a talent, Moore has not been back to Virginia Tech since his playing days ended. The school has tried to have a ceremony to retire his jersey. He has yet to show.

Where is he now?

"I want to say Memphis, but that may not be right," Tech coach Frank Beamer says.

Charley Wiles, the Tech assistant coach in charge of defensive linemen, says Moore called him about two years ago and talked about getting into coaching. Wiles said he'd help, but Moore never got back to him. Reaching Moore, Wiles says, always involves going through a chain of people and leaving messages, some of which are returned.

"Corey was a little bit of a different guy," Wiles says. "He wasn't your typical football player. He was one of those guys who carried a little bit of a chip on his shoulder. He wasn't a guy to open up, to let you in easily. He wasn't real trusting. Where that comes from, I don't know."

Moore's route to Tech was a circuitous one, with Wiles at the center. From Brownsville, Tennessee, Moore caught Wiles' attention when Wiles was an assistant at Murray State. Moore ended up signing with Mississippi. Wiles ended up going to Tech and joining Beamer's staff. But before Moore could play there, Mississippi got a new coach in Tommy Tuberville. Suddenly there was no room for Moore. He ended up going to Holmes

Community College in Goodman, Mississippi. A qualifier out of high school, he re-opened his recruiting. That's where Wiles got involved again.

"I knew we needed another end," Wiles recalls. "He played tight end and defensive end in high school. We had a relationship and we were able to get him."

The Setting

While the need was there for Tech, at 6 feet and barely 200 pounds, Moore wasn't ready to contribute right away. He took a redshirt season, then played as a backup for a year. The following spring, Moore got noticed.

"Corey committed himself," Wiles recalls. "He wanted to be the next great defensive end here. He got bigger; he got really powerful. Two years after he gets here, he's up around 230 pounds. Weight affects different people in different ways. He was able to get bigger and stay as quick as he was, now with more power.

"He came out that spring and we couldn't block him."

Few could. Moore's junior and senior seasons were spectacular. Tech was good in 1998, finishing 8-3 in the regular season before beating Alabama in the inaugural Music City Bowl. Moore was the Big East Conference's defensive player of the year.

"I remember sitting with Corey and Alabama's punter at a luncheon before that bowl," recalls Bill Roth, Tech's longtime play-by-play broadcaster. "Corey said, 'We're probably going to block one of your punts.' The kid said he'd never had a punt blocked. Corey said, 'We'll get one.' We got two, one of them by Corey that led to a touchdown.

"He was a kid who always rose to the occasion. I don't know that we've ever had a player other than Michael Vick who always seemed to play his best when he had to."

Both Tech and Moore had something to prove in a game against Clemson during Moore's senior season. Tech had a strong 1998 campaign, one that ended with the victory over Alabama on a cold, wet night in the Music City Bowl. Moore's defensive player of the year honor in the Big East garnered him a lot of attention going into the 1999 season as a player to watch nationally. Vick, a redshirt freshman, was scheduled to make his debut

Notes on Corey Moore

Name:	Corey Moore
Born:	March 20, 1977
Hometown:	Brownsville, Tennessee
Current residence:	Unknown
Occupation:	Unknown
Position:	Defensive end
Height/Playing weight:	6-0, 230
Years lettered:	1997-99
Accomplishments:	Perhaps the most decorated Hokie ever, Moore won the Lombardi and Nagurski Awards in 1999 when he had 17 sacks and 11 other tackles for loss. He was a unanimous All-American. He was the Big East Conference's defensive player of the year in 1998 and 1999. For his career, Moore had 35 sacks for 292 yards worth of losses.
Nickname:	The Disruptor
The game:	Clemson at Virginia Tech, September 23, 1999

in 1999 at quarterback. This was a team that could be special, with a genuine star on offense in Vick, to complement the defensive star, Moore.

But Tech eased into the start of the 1999 season against inferior competition. Two games in, no one really knew any more about the Hokies than they did before the season started. That's why the Clemson game was big. The Tigers were coming off a very disappointing 3-8 season in 1998, and 1999 didn't start too well when they lost their opener at home to Marshall. The next week, Clemson delivered a whipping to a team Tech knew well. The Tigers routed No. 19 Virginia 33-14. Clemson wasn't a national championship contender. It would, however, be a real test.

Game Results

Thursday night games at Virginia Tech's Lane Stadium provide some of the best collegiate football atmosphere anywhere. Television commentators and newspaper columnists say it all the time. A Thursday night early in the 1999 season was a prime example. Tech fans thought something special was developing. The team had rolled to victories over James Madison and Alabama-Birmingham, hardly the type of teams you could gauge a program against.

Now Clemson was in town, a well-respected team from the Atlantic Coast Conference. This would be a better indicator. The final score, 31-11, was a bit misleading, as Clemson did indeed prove to be a test. With 11:31 to play, the Hokies lead was just 14-11. Two defensive touchdowns in the final 3:09 created the wide gap in points. Moore literally had his hands in both. He pressured Clemson quarterback Brandon Streeter hard, leading to an interception that Ike Charlton returned for a 34-yard touchdown.

Then Moore took the final steps in the game that would help make him a national name. He bore down on Streeter and then made contact. The ball came loose. Moore's quickness enabled him to get off Streeter and onto the ball. He picked it up and headed for the end zone, trying to complete what radio color commentator Mike Burnop called "the hat trick"—a sack, a forced fumble, and a touchdown.

In the game, Moore also had two other tackles behind the line. Beamer called him "the disruptor" because he had the ability to take a team

On a Thursday night against Clemson, Virginia Tech's Corey Moore made a national name for himself.

completely out of its offense. Wiles talked about Moore "making plays everywhere, from sideline to sideline."

"We just couldn't block him," Clemson coach Tommy Bowden said afterward. "He's every bit what he's billed up to be."

Says Beamer: "He just kind of took over that game, particularly in the fourth quarter. It was an unbelievable performance before a national audience, and I know it went a long way toward all the awards and trophies he won. I've never seen a 6-foot guy who was able to take over a game the way he was—he was just so fast coming off that edge."

On the ESPN television broadcast, Lee Corso said, "Give him the Outland Trophy right now." Fellow commentator Kirk Herbstreit said afterward, "That guy is as good as it gets. Right before he made that play [the fumble return for a touchdown], I said, 'You know, we haven't called Corey Moore's name lately,' and all of a sudden he comes up with two huge plays."

On the radio broadcast, Roth called it the most dominating defensive performance at Tech. His partner Burnop agreed. "The greatest game I've ever seen by a defensive player," he said.

Given the wide viewing audience on a Thursday night, the game helped stamp Tech as a serious contender for the national championship. Meanwhile, Moore made all the highlight reels.

Tech went on to an 11-0 regular-season record before losing to Florida State in the Sugar Bowl. Moore collected just about every honor available, becoming the second Tech player to be a unanimous All-American.

Moore—who could be both charming and surly in interviews—caused a stir at the Sugar Bowl with an explosion during a media session, an act some say was contrived to take some of the attention off Vick and some of the other younger Tech players.

"He got weird down there, got a little goofy toward the end," Wiles says, "and I don't know exactly why. He was off the hook a little at the bowl game."

Life After Tech

Following his team's defeat at the hands of Tech, Clemson coach Bowden said, "Good players like [Moore] will themselves to make plays in

Moore never gave Clemson's Brandon Streeter much time to get off a pass.

the fourth quarter." Moore, Bowden said, was "a No. 1 draft pick coming after you."

But it didn't quite work out that way. The Buffalo Bills took Moore with the 89th pick in the NFL draft. A year later, he was with the Miami Dolphins after also being released by Cincinnati. He did more damage in one game as a collegian than he did in his short pro career.

Beamer, Bowden, and Wiles all agree that the problem was simple: The pro folks thought Moore was too small to play on the line, so they tried to make him a linebacker. He wasn't a linebacker. He was an end.

"I thought he'd survive up there as an edge rusher because of technique, aggressiveness, and things like that," Bowden says. "He probably didn't have a feel for linebacker."

Beamer agrees: "I still believe to this day if the pros had just left him down it would have worked."

Wiles' take?

"I wish they'd given him the opportunity to play down," Wiles says. "I know he could have been just like Dwight Freeney. I saw him go against a lot of good players, one of them being [tight end] Bubba Franks from Miami. No one could block him one on one. He'd get off so fast, get under your pads so fast. Corey had never played up before. I think they did him a great disservice by moving him and having him play off the line."

*　*　*

Locating Moore proved to be a fruitless effort. There were rumors a couple of years ago that he was in law school at the University of Virginia— a claim not surprising since Moore was exceptionally bright, earning a degree in finance. But the rumor was not true. The latest is that he's changed his name and is selling real estate in Memphis.

Theories abound about the reason why Moore hasn't returned to Tech. Beamer is among those with a retired jersey. So is Jim Pyne, the first unanimous All-American from the school. Carroll Dale, Bruce Smith, and Frank Loria are some of the others. The school has tried to get Moore back for a ceremony. Some will tell you Moore is mad at the school, though no one seems to know why, if this is indeed true. Others say Moore is embarrassed that he didn't enjoy the same success as a pro that he did as a collegian. Wiles thinks it's a simple matter of Moore just moving on with his life.

"I don't know why he hasn't come back. He's had plenty of opportunities," Wiles says. "I don't know if he thinks he's embarrassed because he didn't go on and have a fantastic NFL career. It doesn't matter to anybody here, to anybody on this staff, that's for sure.

"He was as big in the development of this program as anybody. He came to work every day. He practiced the same way he played. He was a very good student. He gave great effort. He graduated. He did everything we asked him to do.

"Time just rolls on. He's just moved on maybe. He feels like [his time at Tech is in] the past. I think if he looks back on his career at Virginia Tech, it would put a smile on his face. He met a lot of terrific people. He touched a lot of people. We won a couple of championships. He has a degree. Those are great memories."

CHAPTER **14**

SHAYNE GRAHAM

You can kick for years and years and years, as Shayne Graham had done, and never get a chance to make a game-winning kick. A year before the game of his life at West Virginia, Graham got that chance. The circumstances were a bit different. The score was tied, so a miss wouldn't be fatal. But a make would mean victory over Miami at the Orange Bowl.

He missed, from a mere 36 yards. Tech went on to win the game in overtime, which eased Graham's pain considerably. But it didn't change the fact that he missed a 36-yarder that would have won the game.

"I hadn't had a chance for one of those my whole career at Virginia Tech, and I got a kick that was a relatively high-percentage kick," Graham recalls. "What happened on that was I took it for granted. I saw it as too much of a routine kick instead of keeping my focus and concentrating. I didn't do what it took to make it happen. I picked my head up too soon. I started the kick but I didn't finish it.

"The key thing is I didn't get mad. I didn't know if I was going to get a chance in overtime. It's important not to let your emotions get the best of you. When the game was over, it was a long flight home, and I could sit there and think about how much more fun the flight would be if I had made that kick."

The Setting

Graham says he thought after the 1998 bowl victory over Alabama that the following season could be really special. A slew of talent returned, and Vick would be taking over at quarterback after sitting out the '98 season as a redshirt.

"We had great players, but they weren't just great players. They were great leaders. That's tough to have, and we had that," Graham says.

Tech started the 1999 season with seven victories. Every team, it seems, that's on the way to something great has to win at least one game when the engine is sputtering. West Virginia didn't shape up to be that game, as the Mountaineers were 3-5 going into their date with the Hokies. But in college football, sometimes things don't shape up as planned.

Game Results

For much of the game, things worked out as expected. When Shyrone Stith scored on a 6-yard run with 4:59 to play, the Hokies had a 19-7 lead. But then things changed quickly. West Virginia needed only 1:44 to score, getting into the end zone on a 4-yard pass from Brad Lewis to Jerry Porter.

Tech still held a 5-point lead. Now it needed a long drive to eat up a lot of time or, preferably, run out the clock.

"We were a pretty good run out the clock team, and all we had to do was hold on to [the ball]," Tech coach Frank Beamer says.

On the third play of that drive, the unthinkable happened. Stith, who never seemed to fumble, did just that. Boo Sensabaugh recovered for West Virginia, which covered 32 yards quickly to score again as Lewis hit Khori Ivy with an 18-yard pass. West Virginia went for two points but failed. Still, West Virginia led 20-19 with 1:15 to play.

"As soon as Shyrone fumbled, I knew I was going to get the chance," Graham says.

Tech took over on its own 15, with 1:15 left to score the winning points and no timeouts. The Hokies knew one loss would be enough to dash their championship hopes. Vick's first pass of the drive fell incomplete. He then found Terrell Parham for 14 yards on the next pass and Andre Davis for nine

Notes on Shayne Graham

Name:	Michael Shayne Graham
Born:	December 9, 1977
Hometown:	Pulaski County, Virginia
Current residence:	Pulaski County, Virginia and Cincinnati, Ohio
Occupation:	Kicker, Cincinnati Bengals
Position:	Kicker
Height/Playing weight:	6-0, 205
Years lettered:	1996-99
Accomplishments:	A regular for four seasons, Graham holds the Tech record for most career points with 371. He led the team in scoring in 1997, 98 and 99. For his career, Graham made 68 of 93 field goal attempts and his streak of 97 straight point-after kicks is a school record. Graham made the all-Big East team four times. Now a professional, he kicked in the 2006 Pro Bowl.
The game:	Virginia Tech at West Virginia, November 6, 1999

yards on the next. Then came Vick's scramble up the sideline, a 26-yard gain that confirmed the Hokies would at least get a chance to kick.

"A great run," Graham says of Vick's play. "What that run did was solidify that I should go ahead and strap up my helmet. There's a piece of video of that run. You can see me on the sideline waiting to see what was going on. You can see me strap my chin strap and go back to the net."

As Graham returned to the practice net to kick a few more balls, Tech tried to advance a little closer to the goal. Graham had connected from 52 yards a week earlier against Pittsburgh, and had a 53-yarder the previous year. But closer is always better.

Vick found Ricky Hall for nine yards. Time was quickly running out. Vick spiked the ball to stop the clock with the Hokies on the West Virginia 27. That meant the kick would have to come from 44 yards.

Beamer nodded at his kicker. It was time. As a four-year regular who was all-league every year, Graham had earned the trust of his coach. Based on weather conditions, the condition of the field, how he felt that day, and other factors, Graham would let Beamer know exactly how far the Hokies would have to get for him to be able to make a field goal. On this day, Graham felt comfortable anywhere from 57 yards in; 44 yards would do just fine.

Graham trotted onto the field with the rest of the field goal unit, knowing a successful kick was necessary if the Hokies were going to realize their dream of playing for a national championship. This kick would keep them unbeaten.

"I wasn't worried about Shayne," Beamer says. "I was more worried about other parts of the operation. If the snap is a little off, if the hold is not quite right … if somebody messes up just a little in protection, you are done."

Cliff Anders was the snapper, Caleb Hurd the holder. Hurd held for Graham in high school, too. The two were very comfortable together. Hurd, now a member of NASCAR driver Jeff Gordon's pit crew, remembers feeling confident and anxious at the same time.

"I knew Shayne wanted it real bad because of the year before at Miami," Hurd says. "I had confidence in him that if we had another chance, he was going to make it.

Shayne Graham wanted a chance as a senior to make up for a missed game-winning kick during his junior season.

"I remember it was not as nerve-wracking as I thought it was going to be. We ran out just like it was any other kick, but everything was happening so fast and we didn't have time to think about it. I did think [about dropping the snap]. All I could think was, 'I cannot be the person they remember from this whole kick.' As long as no one knew who I was, I'd be okay."

West Virginia called timeout in an attempt to "ice" the kicker. It had the opposite effect. Graham, Hurd, and teammates used the break to calm themselves and prepare to do something they had done countless times before.

"We ran out there, we got the spot, we were getting ready, and [West Virginia] called timeout," recalls Graham. "It was almost a sigh of relief. I had a chance to get my heart rate slowed down. ... We would have been fine either way, but that timeout gave us a chance to catch our breath, get under control. The trainers came out and gave us water. We had smiles on our faces. We were very comfortable.

"I don't remember the exact dialogue, but 'cake' [as in 'piece of cake'] was the word that came out of my mouth. I don't know why. It sounds like a very cocky thing to say. ... That was the phrase that came out before the kick. I don't even know if Caleb heard it.

"I also remember the smells of that moment. That was one of the best moments of my sports career. I remember the smells coming off from behind the bleachers, they were grilling something over there and you could see the smoke rising up. I took it all in during those moments."

When they finally lined up for the kick, Graham cleared his head and concentrated on his spot, marked by Hurd's finger. Anders' snap was perfect. Hurd caught it cleanly and got it down. Graham put his foot on the ball and kept his head down. The stadium stayed mostly silent, a good sign. Graham didn't really need to hear anything other than the sound of his foot on the ball.

He knew: He didn't miss this time. The ball sailed cleanly through with room to spare. Tech was still unbeaten.

"When you hit the ball, there's a feeling like [when you strike] a golf ball, a baseball ... you definitely know when there's good contact. It's almost like you don't feel it, it feels so clean," Graham says. "That's how it was. It had the perfect sound, that deep solid sound. Caleb knows that just as well as I do. We both felt it as soon as we hit it.

Graham steps into the kick that beat West Virginia and kept Virginia Tech unbeaten.

"I threw my hands up and turned, and all I saw was the West Virginia sideline and Caleb. He was beside me. Then I started getting pushed and mauled by guys, kind of like a mosh pit. I wish whoever decided to pick me up did it with a little more leverage. They were above my waist.

"It was a little uncomfortable but probably the best I've felt while being uncomfortable."

Hurd said he did know as soon as Graham's foot knocked the ball out of his hold. He took a quick peek to make sure and then searched out Graham.

"It really gave us a lot of confidence that we could handle anything," Hurd says. "That was the first time we'd had a close game all year, and to know we could handle adversity made us feel a lot better."

Broadcaster Bill Roth agrees: "Every great team has that one game where it has to figure out how to win. I knew after Shayne made that kick we wouldn't lose."

Tech didn't lose during the regular season, earning the team a trip to the Sugar Bowl, where it lost to Florida State in the game for the national championship. They wouldn't have made it to New Orleans if not for

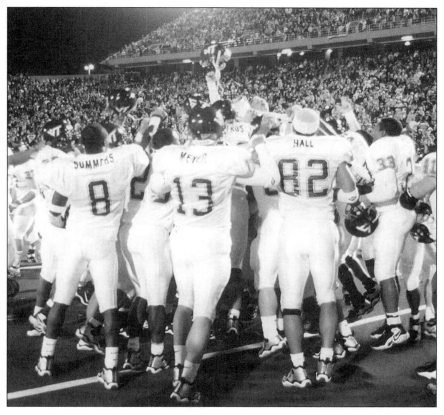

Teammates mob Graham after his 44-yard field goal at the horn provided the winning points at West Virginia.

Graham's 44-yarder. Though he'd been an excellent kicker for a long time, that one kick elevated Graham's status considerably.

"What it did at first was turn recognition on campus up a little bit," Graham says. "My hometown is basically the Blacksburg area, and that meant a lot to a lot of people where I'm from. I heard that from a lot of people. It seemed like everywhere I'd go people would make a comment about it. It was hard to go places without people knowing who I was, which was cool but weird sometimes.

"We'd never been to the national championship before, and that was the closest thing to taking it away from us. It was a big deal. It was a national, breaking out, spotlight moment."

Reflecting on Tech

It took a while after he left Tech, but Graham has established himself in the NFL, making the 2006 Pro Bowl. He's had game-winning kicks as a professional. But the first ball you see in a display case he has in his home isn't from any pro game.

It's the ball that scored the winning points at West Virginia.

"You always remember your first [game-winner]," Graham says. "You always remember what got you there. That kick had a lot to do with it. It's something that sticks in people's minds, that you can make the pressure kick."

CHAPTER 15

MICHAEL VICK

An interesting debate crops up now and then whenever fans of Virginia Tech gather to talk about what has become one of the nation's most successful programs. The Hokies will go into the 2006 season with a bowl streak that has reached 13 seasons. They've won 11 games in a season three times since 1999. So what's the debate?

What person deserves the most credit for elevating Tech to its current status?

Is it Frank Beamer, the Tech alum who has been the head coach since 1987? Is it Dave Braine, the former Tech athletic director? Or is it Michael Vick? The answer, of course, is all three.

Beamer stuck with the school when he had a chance to leave for Boston College after the 1990 season. He persevered through some difficult times, stuck to his basic beliefs in how a program should be run, and eventually turned Tech into a perennial winner. He is the face of Virginia Tech football, and rightfully so.

Braine did not hire Beamer, as many people think. Beamer was hired by Dutch Baughman, who was hired to clean up a mess left by his predecessor, Bill Dooley. But Baughman didn't stay long. He was on the job less than a year, with the hiring of Beamer his notable move.

Where Braine comes in is with a decision he made after the 1992 season, when the Hokies went 2-8-1 and collapsed in the fourth quarter of five games. Despite plenty of pressure to do otherwise, he made the decision that Beamer was the right coach for the program, and that he would be retained. Tech hasn't missed a bowl game since.

Beamer coached a number of notable players at Tech, but Vick became the first national superstar—a player with a big smile and even bigger skills who played the most glamorous position of all. A lot of people became Virginia Tech fans after they became Michael Vick fans.

"He was magical," says Bill Roth, Tech's radio broadcaster.

From Newport News, Virginia, Vick was well regarded for a prep career that saw him throw for 4,846 yards and 43 touchdowns. He ran for another 18. But he was overshadowed by another star from his area, Ronald Curry, who was being pursued as a football and as a basketball player. Curry went to North Carolina to play football. Vick, somewhat lost in the Curry fanfare, headed to Virginia Tech.

The Setting

At his request, Vick sat out the 1998 season as a redshirt. It was the smart move, a chance to let him get acclimated to college life while Al Clark played out his senior year. Even when Vick was a redshirt, running the scout team, Tech sensed it had a serious star in the making.

"I remember watching practice in 1998," Roth says. "I said, 'I think our scout team quarterback runs the Syracuse offense better than Donovan McNabb.'

"Baseball uses the term 'scoring position.' Wherever we had the ball on the field with Michael out there, we were in scoring position."

The excitement only grew once Vick actually started playing. He was a runner, a thrower, and an improviser. Many coaches said during the season that they were most worried about Vick when things went wrong, not when they went right. Beamer liked to joke that there were two versions of every play in the Hokies' playbook—the one that was called and the one that Vick created.

Roth recalled a play against Temple where Vick was wearing a wristband he'd borrowed from backup quarterback Grant Noel, who was right-handed.

"He calls the play and they break the huddle and everything is inverted," Roth says. "[Offensive coordinator] Rickey Bustle is going, 'What the hell is this, we don't have this play.' Vick ends up going 80 yards for a

Notes on Michael Vick

Name:	Michael Dwayne Vick
Born:	June 26, 1980
Hometown:	Newport News, Virginia
Current residence:	Duluth, Georgia
Occupation:	Quarterback, Atlanta Falcons
Position:	Quarterback
Height/Playing weight:	6-1, 214
Years lettered:	1999-2000
Accomplishments:	Vick crammed an awful lot into his two years in a Hokies uniform. As a redshirt freshman, he finished third in the Heisman Trophy balloting, won an ESPY Award as the nation's top collegiate player, and won the inaugural Archie Griffin Award as the most valuable college football player. He was the Big East Conference's offensive player of the year and rookie of the year and was runner-up in voting for The Associated Press Player of the Year award. The AP named him a second-team All-American, and *The Sporting News* named him to their first team All-America squads. Vick's passing efficiency of 180.37 led Division I-A. He passed for 1,840 yards as a freshman and 1,234 yards as a sophomore. He added 585 rushing yards as a freshman and 617 as a sophomore. Despite playing only two years, he left Tech in seventh place on the school's all-time total offense list with 4,276 yards. He had four games where he ran for more than 100 yards, including a 210-yard game against Boston College as a sophomore. Vick became the No. 1 pick in the 2001 NFL draft.
Nickname:	Superman
The game:	Virginia Tech versus Florida State in the Sugar Bowl, January 4, 2000

touchdown on a play where he's wearing the wrong wristband and everything is backwards."

Plays like that—big plays on what should have been busted—became common as Vick led the Hokies to victory after victory. With each victory, and each new Vick accomplishment, more and more people starting paying attention to the Hokies. A buzz started building—was this team good enough to play for the national championship?

Tech swept all 11 regular-season games and earned a spot opposite Florida State in the Sugar Bowl to determine the national championship. Between the time the regular season ended and the Hokies made the trip to New Orleans, Vick-mania grew. The star quarterback was invited to New York for the Heisman Trophy ceremony. He finished third in the balloting, tied for the highest finish by a freshman. Ron Dayne of Wisconsin won the Heisman, with Joe Hamilton of Georgia Tech the runner-up.

"I knew about the Heisman before this year," Vick told the *Richmond Times-Dispatch* after the awards ceremony. "But you don't really know how big it is until you get up here. It definitely leaves a taste in your mouth."

Said Hamilton: "Time is on Michael's side. I like Mike and his game too much to say he's definitely going to win one or two Heisman trophies. I wouldn't put that kind of pressure on anybody. But as long as Mike's healthy, there won't be a year he can't win it."

Vick didn't win any Heisman trophies. He only stayed at Tech two years, and his second season didn't match his first for statistics or hype. But he had one more big game to play that freshman year, and did he ever play big.

Game Results

Despite its perfect record, Tech wasn't seen as a serious threat to a perennial power like Florida State. The Seminoles were expected to walk to the national championship. And the final score may give the impression they did. Florida State won 46-29. But Tech led as late as the fourth quarter. The game turned into a coming-out party for Vick. Short of actually winning the game, Tech and Vick got as much out of the Sugar Bowl experience as they possibly could.

Michael Vick provided plenty of highlights during his two years in a Virginia Tech uniform.

One play in particular wowed all who witnessed it. The left-handed Vick rolled to his right to attempt to free himself of the bevy of Florida State defenders in pursuit. The Seminoles were quickly learning that the redshirt freshman from Virginia Tech was a lot quicker in person than he looked on film. But this time, the Seminoles seemed to have Vick cornered. He was running out of room, and he wasn't going to be able to turn upfield and go on one of his patented broken-play long runs.

As he was being chased, Vick noticed something way on the other side of the field. Receiver Andre Davis was open, if just barely. This wasn't going to be an easy throw. Vick had to stop quickly and turn. Not only was Davis way downfield, he was just about all the way across the field, too. The opening was about as big as the hole of a tire.

Davis kept sprinting down the field. Down 14-0 early in the game, the Hokies were eager to make something happen quickly. That it was such a difficult throw never even occurred to Vick. He stopped quickly, turned, and fired.

The pass sailed through the air to Davis, who caught it for a 49-yard-first-quarter touchdown that cut the FSU lead to 14-7. The Hokies fell behind 28-7 before rallying behind Vick to go ahead 29-28 late in the third quarter.

But Vick and the Hokies couldn't hold on for the win. Still, they compiled some awe-inspiring totals: Tech collected 503 yards in the game, and Vick accounted for 322 of them. He passed for 225 yards and rushed for 97.

"I knew he was good. I didn't know he was that good," FSU coach Bobby Bowden said after the game.

"And that wasn't Johnny Hopscotch out there on defense trying to chase him down," Roth says. "That was Corey Simon out there. Tech put over 500 yards of offense on the board that night. That was a great Florida State team. You run out of superlatives as a broadcaster—sensational, spectacular, spine-tingling. With Vick, you didn't have enough superlatives."

Despite the loss, no one said after the game that Tech wasn't a legitimate, title-contending team. And everyone was buzzing about the Hokies' amazing quarterback.

"It was a national stage and a whole lot of people were looking and they all went, 'Wow, he really is good.'" Beamer says of Vick. "I went to Houston the next day because I was getting an award down there, and I did an interview on a call-in show. They said all anybody was talking about was not Florida State and the national championship, but this guy Michael Vick. I don't know that there's ever been a time that one game meant so much to a guy's reputation as that game right there."

Vick accounted for 322 yards against Florida State in the Sugar Bowl following the 1999 season.

Among those watching was Bruce Smith, the former Tech standout who became the No. 1 pick in the NFL draft 16 years before Vick. Smith ended up with the NFL record for career sacks.

"That is one special player," he said after the Sugar Bowl. "I wouldn't want to have to chase him down."

Will Stewart, general manager of the TechSideline.com Web-site, summed things up well in his postgame analysis.

"Well, one thing's for sure—all the doubters about Michael Vick are now silenced," Stewart wrote. "You will no longer hear someone comment about how he has built his reputation against JMU, UAB, Rutgers, and Temple. Many observers felt Vick would fold under the pressure of a national championship game combined with the FSU defense.

"Certainly Vick played far from a perfect game … but he made some incredible plays and, most importantly, he never wilted.

"Vick blew the minds of all who watched the game. Peter Warrick was the MVP of the bowl, but Vick made more highlight-film plays."

It wasn't an easy night for Vick. Florida State did sack him seven times. He also lost those two fumbles.

"I got knocked around more than I ever have in a football game," Vick said after the game. "I did everything in my power I could. I tried to get away from people, tried to make tough throws, took so many hits.

"We did a lot of things in the second half. We made plays, got some points, and jumped ahead. We showed everybody that we could come back. … In my heart, we are still champions."

Vick's teammates enjoyed watching him as much as Florida State hated chasing him.

"Seeing Mike running around out there against Florida State, making them look so silly, you started realizing how special Mike was," defensive tackle David Pugh said. "FSU has some of the best athletes in the nation. Mike personally tore two ACLs in that game of guys trying to chase him."

* * *

Tech fans didn't have to worry about Vick bolting after his redshirt freshman season. The current rules say a player can't turn pro until he's been out of high school for three years. Plus, Vick knew he needed more time in

If he didn't beat you with his feet, Vick could do it with his arm.

college, and he enjoyed being there. The following year, the decision was more difficult. Before the team left for the Gator Bowl after his sophomore season, Vick actually stood before the assembled press and said he would return for another season. No one believed it and, sure enough, Vick let slip in a pre-Gator Bowl interview that he was thinking of leaving when the season was complete. He really had no choice.

Vick's family was not one of means, and everyone expected him to be the first player taken in the draft. He could take out insurance against injury and stay another year, but the financial risk was still too big.

"[Color commentator] Mike Burnop and I were talking with Michael before the Gator Bowl," Roth recalls. "We asked him, 'What are you really going to do?' He asked me, 'What would you do?' [I told him] 'I'd call Peyton Manning, Donovan McNabb—the other guys who stayed.' He said he'd talked with a lot of people, and they thought he could be the No. 1 pick overall. It would be worth 20-25 million.

"I said, 'This isn't really a tough decision.' He ended up getting $30 million."

As much as they would have liked to have seen Vick stay another year, no one at Tech could begrudge his decision. He'd left quite a mark in his two years under center, and lifted the Hokies to a serious national championship contender. He also left quite an impression on those he played against, and with.

"Mike basically took the skills that a lot of players have and added his gift of athleticism to that," says Shayne Graham, the Hokies' kicker during Vick's freshman season and now a fellow Pro Bowl player. "He did something not everybody can do. He could make the best out of a bad situation. Half the time he ran the ball it was because he was about to get sacked. He could turn a six-yard loss into an 80-yard touchdown.

"He did things that were, for the most part, inhuman. That's how he got the nickname Superman. He did things the normal man couldn't do and did a super job doing them."

CHAPTER 16

ANDRE DAVIS

Andre Davis was no different from most kids. He wanted to be a professional athlete, and he wanted to go to the Olympics. He thought he could achieve both goals, but not as a football player; Davis played soccer.

"Football wasn't even on the radar," Davis says. "I thought I was pretty good at soccer, and I enjoyed the time that I played. It just didn't work out.

"I'm glad it didn't work out."

So are a lot of Virginia Tech football fans. A suggested move from the offensive end of the soccer field to the defensive end didn't sit well with Davis. He had some friends who played football and they suggested he give that a try. His speed would come in handy and he could even use his hands. Davis' friends were right. In two short years, he did well enough that he knew football was something he wanted to continue doing.

Finding a place to do it was another story. Several schools on the Division I-AA level wanted him to play for them, and Davis would have had no problem playing at that level.

"Just the idea that they would pay for me to go to school was good enough," Davis says. "I was just grateful to have that chance."

Before he signed with one of those schools, however, Davis wanted to give something a try. His cousin, Richard Bowen, played at a school a good bit away from Davis' home in upstate New York. Virginia Tech was starting to emerge as a big-time player in the college football world. Maybe he wasn't good enough to play there, but Davis didn't think it would hurt to inquire. He sent a tape to Bowen and asked him to show it to Tech's coaches.

"It was interesting," Tech coach Frank Beamer recalls of the tape. "We took a look, and I never will forget him catching a ball across the middle and turning it on like we eventually saw him do so many times here.

"He didn't have a lot of film and he didn't have a lot of catches. I remember saying, 'You know, if he can do that one time he can do it every time,' so we ended up recruiting him. He was a smart guy, and you saw him getting better all the time. I liked what he was all about."

Even Davis' recruiting visit wasn't traditional. He and his parents were on an official visit to the University of Delaware when they decided to keep driving south when it was over to check out Tech. Davis liked what he saw.

"Tech had an opportunity to go to a Sugar Bowl, to play Texas," says Davis, who would later play in a Sugar Bowl himself against Florida State. "This was a program on the rise, a team that was getting more and more television time. I figured if I was going to have an opportunity to play pro ball, my chances would be better [at Tech]. On my visit, there was no hoopla at all. I didn't get a chance to see any other players. We got a tour of campus, went to dinner, and that was it."

It was enough. Davis' mind was made up—he was coming to Tech.

The Setting

Davis quickly proved to be possibly the best "unknown" recruit in the history of the program. Tech saw it had a very bright, polite, engaging, young man who had two other pretty important traits—speed and a work ethic.

"Andre didn't just become a football player," says Bill Roth, the longtime radio voice of the Hokies. "He really worked hard to become a sensational receiver. It wasn't luck."

Defensive tackle and teammate David Pugh adds: "The best thing about Andre, regardless of how many touchdowns he scored, he's just a great guy on and off the field. He wasn't a party guy. He was just a guy you'd take home to meet your mom and dad, and they would just love him."

Tech is not known as a receivers school, and there's a good reason for that: The Hokies never had a receiver catch as many as 50 passes in a season until Ernest Wilford did it in 2002. Davis led the team in receiving two years, but in either season he didn't catch as many as 40 passes. For his career,

Notes on Andre Davis

Name:	Andre Nathaniel Davis
Born:	June 12, 1979
Hometown:	Niskayuma, New York
Current residence:	Miami, Florida
Occupation:	Receiver with the Buffalo Bills. Davis joined the Bills after the 2005 season after spending three seasons with the Cleveland Browns, who drafted him with the 47th overall pick in the 2002 NFL draft, and one with the New England Patriots.
Position:	Receiver
Height/Playing weight:	6-1, 195
Years lettered:	1998-2001
Accomplishments:	Davis was a talented receiver and return man for the Hokies. The American Football Coaches Association named him to its All-America team as a return man in 2000, the season he returned 18 punts for a school-record average of 22 yards. He tied a record by returning three of them for touchdowns. Davis led Tech in receiving in 1999 and 2001. He finished his career with 103 catches for 1,986 yards and 18 touchdowns.
The game:	West Virginia at Virginia Tech, October 12, 2000

he caught 103 passes. By comparison, Mike Williams had 95 catches in 2003 at Southern California.

Tech receivers did take note of the discrepancy.

"Oh definitely," Davis says. "As I was going through college, I was looking at schools like Florida, seeing three guys having 60-plus catches and their running back having 1,000 yards. I was like, 'Why can't we do that, too?'

"But there's another side to that. Tech was a run-first team. Anytime you're a leading receiver on a team like that, you're going to get noticed. When you have a team that has success, full of team players and guys not worried about stats, it brings everything together and helps them be successful. Success gets you noticed, too."

Tech may not be Receiver U, but there is a list of talented receivers who have played for the Hokies and then played professionally, including Antonio Freeman, Wilford, Davis, and Bryan Still.

Davis had his opportunity to shine in a home matchup against West Virginia during his junior year.

Game Results

The Hokies defeated the Mountaineers 48-20, a victory that wasn't nearly as easy as the final score would lead one to believe, considering that West Virginia led 14-7 at halftime. Michael Vick helped erase that deficit early in the second half when he connected with tight end Bob Slowikowski on a 72-yard touchdown pass. After that, it became the Davis show.

Davis had what Roth calls "the three greatest touches in Lane Stadium history." With 8:30 left in the third quarter, the Hokies called for an end around. Davis made it work for a 30-yard touchdown. When they got the ball back, the Hokies decided to go deep again. This time, Vick hooked up with Davis for a 64-yard touchdown pass with 4:20 to play in the quarter. It came after West Virginia had tried—and failed—to convert on a fourth-down-and-three play.

Don Nehlen, West Virginia's coach at the time, said there was nothing complicated about that play. Davis simply lined up and ran past his defensive backs. Davis doesn't disagree.

As a youngster, Andre Davis thought his future was in soccer, not football.

"That's pretty much all it was," he says. "A lot of times in college if I knew I could outrun somebody, I'd take off running and tell Michael to throw it as far as he could and I'd go get it. It was a perfectly thrown ball. I caught it right in stride and took it right into the end zone. It was just something to keep us rolling."

But Davis wasn't done yet. He saved the best for last. Tech forced a punt on West Virginia's next possession. And with that, it was time for Act III of The Davis Show.

As well as he did as a receiver at Virginia Tech, Davis was perhaps even more dangerous returning kicks. In fact, he'd go on to make some All-America teams with his return skills. As the punt flew through the air toward him, he knew it was one that could be returned. The ball settled softly in his hands and he took off. Like many long, successful returns, this one came down to a single man standing between Davis and the end zone. With his speed, Davis might have been able to do it himself. But it never hurts to have help. Out of the corner of his eye, Davis saw teammate Wayne Ward. A running back by trade, almost all of Ward's playing time came on special teams. He was popular with his teammates and he was about to become part of Tech folklore—and help Davis do the same.

Davis heard a tremendous roar from the full house at Lane Stadium. He still had a long way to go to get into the end zone, so he knew they were cheering for Ward's hit on Mountaineer Kyle Kayden. A few seconds later, Davis found himself in the end zone again, this time with a 76-yard punt return.

"I remember setting the guy up, and I think I saw Wayne coming around for the hit," recalls Davis. "I really wished I could have turned around and seen the hit. But I realized then that I had the whole sideline, and I knew I was going to score from there.

"When [the play] was over, all I wanted to do was run back and find Wayne after that. I finally saw [the hit] later that night when we were watching *SportsCenter*. What a hit."

The hit was remarkable, but so was the touchdown, Davis' third of the day.

"In a little less than seven minutes, he kind of established himself and probably made himself a lot of money in the NFL," Beamer says.

Pugh adds: "It was unbelievable … the block Wayne put on that guy sticks out in my mind. If Andre gets out in the open, he's gone. You're talking to a guy who never scored a touchdown. I can't imagine what it feels like to score three that quick."

Davis ended up touching the ball 11 times that night, good for 273 yards and the three touchdowns. He had six catches for 127 yards, four punt returns for 116 yards, and the one rush for 30 yards.

In one quarter against West Virginia, Davis scored three touchdowns three different ways.

Life After Tech

"That game has definitely helped my career," Davis says. "That was one of those games I could just show everybody that I could be dangerous in all parts of my game.

"I'm trying to make some new highlights now [in the NFL], but that was one great night. During the game, I don't think I really realized all that was happening. You're just so focused on the game, trying to get the win. It wasn't until later that I realized how special it was."

CHAPTER 17

DAVID PUGH

In its 2002 draft preview, the website NFL.com describes David Pugh as a "good, old country-boy type who simply loves to play the game." Truer words have never been spoken. Pugh loved to go fishing with fellow defensive tackle and pal Chad Beasley. He was a country boy and proud of it. But what he really loved was playing football. And proving people wrong.

At 6 feet, 3 inches, and 271 pounds, Pugh wasn't very big in the world of football trenches.

"I used to kid him, tell him not to get off the bus first," Tech coach Frank Beamer says. "Those offensive linemen might get their confidence up. He's not an imposing guy."

He had a stellar high school career but wasn't heavily recruited. Some of that had to do with his size. More of it had to do with the fact that he decided early he was going to Virginia Tech, barely two hours away from home.

"Virginia Tech kind of caught me right after my junior year," Pugh says. "They had been looking at film of another guy and noticed me. I committed to Tech so early that a lot of people didn't jump on me. I was getting letters and talking to people, but I wouldn't say I was a huge recruit. I do think I would have had opportunities to go to other Division I schools.

"[Coach] Mickey Crouch told me they were looking at me, and he told me it was the perfect place for me, that'd I'd love it down there. It wasn't that far [from home], they had the mountains all around … he said I'd love it. I didn't pay a lot of attention to college football growing up, so it was all new to me. I did see them play in the Orange Bowl one year and the Sugar Bowl the next. That was pretty impressive. I never wanted to go to Virginia. Coach Crouch was right—it was a perfect fit for me."

It was perfect for another reason: Tech never put a premium on size, especially on defense. Defensive coordinator Bud Foster has always been a speed-first guy. If someone had size *and* speed, so much the better. But someone who had the strength and quickness of Pugh would get a fair shot.

"What's the use of being 350 pounds if you can't move?" Pugh says. "If you can get a guy who is 300 and runs a 4.8 [for 40 yards], that's great. They don't come along too often. I've been called undersized. I don't refer to myself as that. For what I lacked in size, I made up for with speed and quickness.

"That was my whole game, getting off the ball before they did. If you can get off the ball before they do, their whole advantage is taken away. To me, size is overrated. If a guy is bigger, it doesn't mean he's stronger. A big guy, that doesn't mean he's going to be able to play. Lots of guys look like Tarzan and play like Jane. I gave up a lot of size, but I'm not the only one who's done that."

The Setting

Pugh stepped into a good program and made a quick impact. He almost didn't take a redshirt season. He was voted newcomer of the year in the spring game the following year, and became a regular in the defensive line rotation in 1998.

"When you play second team on the defensive line, you're still going to play a lot of snaps," he says. "I felt like I was ready. I didn't feel any pressure. Chad Beasley became the other tackle by the time we became starters, and we were a good combination. You had one big guy who could clog up the middle a little more. I liked to consider myself more of a disruptor. What Chad lacked I had … what I lacked, he had."

Defensive line coach Charley Wiles has been at Tech 10 years and has coached a number of linemen who have gone on to the NFL. He says Pugh is "probably the best defensive tackle that I coached here. … It's kind of funny in recruiting, where everybody projects different guys to do different things. He was projected as an offensive lineman with the opportunity to

Notes on David Pugh

Name:	David Winston Pugh Jr.
Born:	July 24, 1979
Hometown:	Madison Heights, Virginia
Current residence:	Madison Heights, Virginia
Occupation:	His NFL career recently ended, and Pugh is looking to get into coaching, possibly at Virginia Tech.
Position:	Defensive tackle
Height/Playing weight:	6-3, 270
Years lettered:	1998-2000
Accomplishments:	Pugh was a durable, dependable defensive lineman who started every game his final two seasons after playing in every game as a reserve his first two seasons. He made the all-Big East Conference team as a junior and senior and was a third-team All-America as a senior. He had 13.5 sacks and 41 total tackles for losses among his 170 career tackles. Pugh was a sixth-round draft choice of the Indianapolis Colts in the 2002 NFl draft.
The game:	Clemson versus Virginia Tech in the Gator Bowl, January 1, 2001

play defense. It turns out he was one of the best and most productive defensive tackles to play here. He had great quickness, great instincts. He was a very flexible guy, he played with a natural bend to his knees. He played underneath people. He had pop. Certain guys have that, they're great hitters. You see a lot of big, strong guys that don't have that great hitting power. He had great timing, too. You teach him a few things and he's smart enough to process what's happening to him and do it quickly. Some guys can't figure it out. They see it on video, but when it is happening on the field it doesn't process. For David, the game made sense."

The year 2001 opened crisp and clear for the Virginia Tech Hokies, who were in Jacksonville, Florida, to play Clemson in the Gator Bowl. They had no time to celebrate on New Year's Eve. The game kicked off at noon on New Year's Day.

Tech wasn't real happy to be there, no offense to the fine folks in Jacksonville and those who run the Gator Bowl. A year earlier, the Hokies were 11-0 in the regular season and lost the Sugar Bowl for the national championship to Florida State. This season, they went 10-1 during the regular season. The Hokies' only loss came at Miami on a day when sophomore quarterback Michael Vick was limited to a handful of plays by an ankle injury. Tech thought it should've been in a Bowl Championship Series game as an at-large selection. The bid the Hokies thought they should get went to Notre Dame instead.

"Everybody felt we had something to prove. We felt like we got the shaft; we only lost one game and thought we should have been in a BCS game," says Pugh. "Instead, Notre Dame went and got embarrassed by Oregon State. We had a chip on our shoulder. People thought we were just second rate compared to them. ... I'm glad they got beat. I think we deserved to go."

In Clemson, Tech was playing a team with an athletic quarterback of its own in Woody Dantzler. He was a guy who could give an opponent fits out of the team's hurried-up, no-huddle offense. The Tigers were confident coming in that they could move the ball on the Hokies. But come game time, they smacked right into reality.

David Pugh used technique and quickness to make up for his relative lack of size.

Game Results

Clemson took the opening kickoff. On the first play, before Dantzler could even get comfortable, the Tech defensive line—led by Pugh—showed him it had other ideas about just how much damage Clemson would do that day. Pugh pressured Dantzler on first down, and the Tigers ended up gaining no yards. Clemson was forced to punt after three plays. A bad snap by the Tigers' Henry Owen was dropped by Jamie Somaini, and the Hokies tackled him on the Clemson 23. It took Vick just one play to get Tech into the end zone, finding Jarrett Ferguson with a scoring pass.

Clemson's next possession? No gain on the first play; a Pugh sack on the second play; and Dantzler was chased on the third play. Pugh ended up with another quarterback "hurry" on the first play of Clemson's next drive. Three possessions in, and Clemson knew its game plan was useless, thanks to the rush that Pugh led.

"I could tell their morale, after that first series, was low," Pugh recalls. "They were hanging their heads. It was almost like they didn't want to be out there. They couldn't stop us.

"One play I really enjoyed, I didn't sack Dantzler, but he rolled to his left and I was on him, chasing him. It was only me out there with him in the open field. He had plenty of places to run and he couldn't duck me. Here's Woody Dantzler, he's supposed to be like a Michael Vick, and he can't even get away from me.

"To me, the Clemson offense was pretty simple. If you could read the blocking schemes correctly, it was relatively easy to decipher. We never let them get going to where they could run that two-minute offense. They were never able to do that, which kept us fresh. Woody is a good athlete, but it seemed like I was step for step with him a lot of the time."

Pugh's official statistics from the game weren't that impressive. He only had five tackles and one sack. But it only took a simple viewing of the game to see how much he controlled things. He was in Clemson's backfield most of the day, forcing a play for someone else if he wasn't making it himself.

"I remember David taking that Gator Bowl over," says Bill Roth, Tech's radio broadcaster. "He dominated that game."

The Hokies 41-20 defeat of Clemson in the Gator Bowl ended up being Michael Vick's last game at Tech. Even though he said at a press

Clemson's Woody Dantzler saw a lot of Pugh during the 2001 Gator Bowl.

conference a couple of weeks before the game that he was going to stay at Tech for another year, he declared for the NFL draft. It was a good move, as he ended up being the No. 1 overall pick. He was named the Most Valuable Player in his final collegiate game, although Pugh may have been a better choice for the award.

Winning that game gave Tech back-to-back seasons with 11-1 records. They were the first two 11-victory seasons in Tech history.

Life After Tech

Pugh stuck with the Indianapolis Colts, but a knee injury suffered during an off-season pickup basketball game scuttled his career. Though he's no longer playing, Pugh has no interest in leaving the game. He plans to become a coach.

"Football has been very good to me," Pugh says. "I've been lucky in all my sports—never really played on any losing teams. I had a great college football career, and I got to play in the league for a few years. That got cut short by injury, but that's the way it goes. I wish I was still playing, but you can't sit around and wish and hope, you just have to move on."

CHAPTER 18

ERNEST WILFORD

Miami's Hurricanes came to Blacksburg thinking roses. They were unbeaten in their first year under coach Larry Coker and knew they had a team good enough to win the national championship, which was going to be decided that year at the Rose Bowl. They also knew that getting out of Blacksburg still unbeaten wasn't going to be easy.

Miami dominated the Hokies. They intercepted Grant Noel four times and sacked him five times. The numbers made it look as if it should be a runaway. Yet it was nothing of the sort. Down 16 points midway through the fourth quarter, Tech found a little life when fullback Jarrett Ferguson scored on a 1-yard run with 8:33 to play. Noel's pass to Terrell Parham on the conversion play was good, and now it was only an eight-point ballgame.

The Hokies' defense held and Miami came out to punt. That's a nail-biting experience for any opposing coach, given Tech's well-earned reputation as a kick-blocking unit. Coker held his breath as the ball was snapped to punter Freddie Capshaw. The crowd at Lane Stadium roared after the telltale second quick "thunk"—the first from the kick and the second from the block. The Hokies' Eric Green blocked the kick. Brandon Manning picked it up cleanly and ran 22 yards for a touchdown. With 6:03 on the clock, the score was 26-24, Miami.

The decision to go for two points again was an easy one. Noel, having one of the worst days in what would be his only full year as the team's starter, dropped back and surveyed the end zone. Alone in the right corner stood Ernest Wilford, a sophomore who had just 10 catches on the season going into the game. He threw an easy pass in Wilford's direction. Wilford's eyes locked on the ball as the crowd got giddy in anticipation of the score being tied going into the closing minutes.

There's no need to build up any suspense. Wilford dropped that pass. Tech got one more chance, Noel was intercepted again, and Miami left Blacksburg unbeaten, then went on to win the Rose Bowl and the national championship. It was by far the most difficult and disappointing day athletically in Wilford's young life.

And this is the game of his life? A bitter disappointment that led to a lot of soul-searching, dealing with a lot of negative response that included a public run-in with Spike Lee? Why, yes, it is indeed. Without that drop, Wilford concedes, he might not be the professional receiver he is now.

When the disappointment eased, Wilford made a simple vow to himself: He would never allow himself to be in a situation where he felt that way again. He would do whatever it took to get over it and become the best receiver he could be.

"I wasn't going to let it beat me," Wilford says. "No way."

Tony Ball, Tech's receivers coach at the time, says, "He took a negative situation and made it a very positive and motivating situation."

Mike Burnop, the man whose record Wilford eventually broke, works as the color commentator on the Hokies' radio network. He calls the drop "a huge turning point for Ernest. It was incredible what he did after that." Over his final two seasons, Wilford caught 106 of his 126 career catches. He became the first Tech receiver to ever catch as many as 50 passes in a season as a junior, and then did it again as a senior. He became a team leader and remains one of the most respected Hokies ever. He became a pro.

He still remembers details of the drop vividly.

"I remember the special teams play, the blocked punt, and touchdown, me jumping around on the field," recalls Wilford. "I knew they'd need me for the two-point conversion.

"[The pass] came at me like it was in slow motion. I was debating how to catch the ball—should I catch it with my hands or my body? I'm a hands catcher. Every time I catch it with my body bad things happen. I didn't go with my gut. It went right through and slipped through my arms, legs, and everything, and just hit the ground. It was a very catchable ball, and I wasn't very fundamentally sound that day.

Notes on Ernest Wilford

Name:	Ernest Lee Wilford Jr.
Born:	January 14, 1979
Hometown:	Richmond, Virginia
Current residence:	Richmond, Virginia and Jacksonville, Florida
Occupation:	On the roster of the Jacksonville Jaguars, who took him in the fourth round of the 2004 NFL draft.
Position:	Wide receiver
Height/Playing weight:	6-4, 225
Years lettered:	2000-03
Accomplishments:	In 2002, Wilford became the first Tech player ever to catch as many as 50 passes in a season when he caught 51. That broke Mike Burnop's record of 46 that had stood since 1971. Wilford followed it up the next year by catching 55 passes to become the Hokies' all-time leading receiver with 126 passes—106 of them coming his final two seasons. His career catches went for 2,052 yards and 11 touchdowns.
The game:	Miami at Virginia Tech, December 1, 2001

"At first I thought I actually caught it. When you watch the replay, you see that it did hit the ground first. Once I saw the ref saying no, I knew I'd lost the game for Virginia Tech."

Wilford was devastated. He didn't meet with the media afterward, though his teammates were supportive.

"That was one play," Noel said. "Without my numerous bad plays, we wouldn't have been in that situation."

Wilford met with Ball the next day.

"I think how I approached it made him feel better," Ball says. "Had I been negative or distraught, it probably would have gone on longer. I wasn't. I wanted to look at why he dropped it and what I could do to help him. That's how I approached it.

"I told him if I had to do it again just like that, I would do it again. How we approached it the day after was the motivating force that got him to where he is. He became a much more disciplined, determined receiver. He worked extremely hard. He didn't want it to happen again, and he understood at that point what it meant to work on something. When he came back [the next season], there wasn't a dropped ball in preseason. Off balance? He made those catches. The driving force was what happened in that Miami game."

Fans were supportive, for the most part, Wilford says.

"There was a negative side to some of the e-mails," he says. "People thought I couldn't play the game, that I'd blown the whole season. I'm lucky I had great coaches who saw me not only as an athlete but as a human being with real feelings. They let me know there was time to make up for it."

The best and worst of the reaction came later that school year, when film director Spike Lee gave a talk on campus. Wilford was in attendance and Lee actually asked the audience, "Where's the guy who dropped that pass?"

Wilford, his confidence rebuilt, never hesitated. "Right here," he said.

"People got all kinds of upset with [Lee]," Wilford recalls with a laugh. "They were hollering at him, one guy even gave him the finger and walked out. ... After the program he asked to see me, and he apologized to me and wished me luck the rest of my career."

Wilford believes that everything happens for a reason—even that dropped pass.

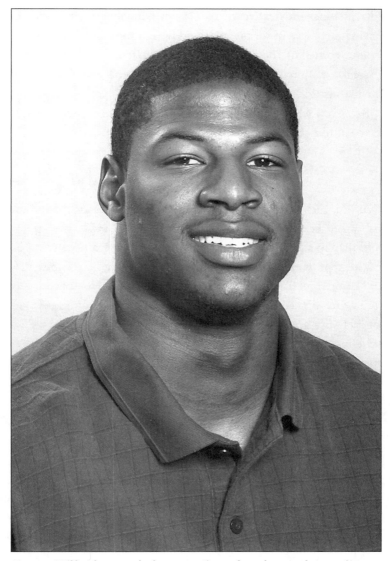

Ernest Wilford turned the negative of a dropped pass into a positive that drove him to a pro career.

"I remember the next year we were down at Miami, and Bryan Randall got hurt. Grant came in for one play and we ran the exact same play into the exact same corner of the end zone. Same quarterback, same spot on the field," recalls Wilford. "He threw it up there, and I made sure I caught it with my hands this time.

"It wasn't a winning play, but it was an important catch, to be able to bounce back like that."

Life After Tech

Wilford said he's still a little amazed when he sees his name atop the Hokies' career receiving list. He had hopes as his Tech career progressed that he could play in the NFL. But he knew it wasn't a certainty.

So he kept working. His attitude and work ethic have endeared him to Jaguar Nation much as they did to Hokie Nation. He's become a major contributor to the team and immersed himself in the community. He is the host of a charity golf tournament—a big deal for a relatively new golfer—that benefits First Tee, an organization that makes golf accessible to kids who otherwise wouldn't have access to the sport.

"Golf is a new hobby that keeps me off the streets," Wilford says. "It really helps my football, the concentration and the mental approach you have to have. When I get a hold of one, I can rip it. I might not know which way it is going, but I can rip it.

"We're trying to help kids who can't afford to play golf to have that opportunity. We want them to learn the values of character, honesty, integrity, and trust. Those are the things I believe in my everyday walk of life, and that's why I chose that organization."

The Jaguars are an organization glad they chose Wilford. When the pass against Miami hit the ground, the last thing Wilford envisioned was getting a call from an NFL team saying it had drafted him. What he did after that dropped pass, however, made that call happen.

"I talked to [coach] Jack Del Rio and thanked him for the opportunity," Wilford says. "I promised him that nobody at the stadium would outwork me.

Wilford became the first Virginia Tech receiver to catch as many as 50 passes in a season, and then did it again the next season.

"There are probably better athletes out there, but I made that commitment that every day I was going to give the Jacksonville Jaguars organization 100 percent—in the community and in everything I do."

Wilford may be devoting 100 percent to the NFL now, but he hasn't forgotten his roots.

"I think back on my days at Virginia Tech every single day," he says. "People are always asking me what makes me tick, what gets me going, what motivates me, and I go back to my days at Virginia Tech and before that at Franklin Military Academy. I let people know where I've been and what it has done for me."

CHAPTER 19

LEE SUGGS

Shyrone Stith gave up his final year of eligibility at Virginia Tech after the 1999 season. The decision came against the advice of many people, and it caused a lot of angst among Hokies fans. Was anybody ready to be the next featured tailback?

Little did anyone know there was someone who was going to be more than ready. Lee Suggs could understand if no one believed that right after Stith decided to leave. He hadn't done anything yet. He was a much-heralded recruit out of William Fleming High in nearby Roanoke, Virginia, where he rushed for 2,918 yards and 30 touchdowns as a senior. He had 5,056 career yards, and was the 19th-best running back prospect in the country, according to one scouting magazine.

But Suggs had yet to show his stuff on the collegiate level, not that he really had much of a chance. He sat out 1998 as a redshirt. In 1999, when Tech advanced to the Sugar Bowl to play Florida State for the national championship, Suggs only carried 44 times for 136 yards. Was he another high school phenom who couldn't carry it over to the collegiate level? Some wondered. Suggs did not.

"When Shyrone left, everybody said, 'We don't have anybody else,'" recalls Billy Hite, Tech's longtime assistant in charge of running backs. "Lee did all the things he needed to do in an eight-month period to get himself ready."

Suggs adds: "I was confident I could be a good back at the Division I level. I never dreamed about setting all those records, scoring all those touchdowns. I just wanted to be a good, solid player."

By the time the 2000 season had ended, Suggs had scored 28 touchdowns—twice the previous school record. He was the Big East Conference's co-offensive player of the year, and a unanimous choice for the Dudley Award, given to the player of the year in the state of Virginia. And he was just a sophomore, with two full years to play.

The next year lasted less than three quarters. Shortly after halftime of the Hokies' opener against Connecticut, Suggs blew out his left knee. He was on his way to another typical Suggs game. He gained 99 yards and scored two touchdowns. But his year was over, before it ever really began.

"The hardest part about sitting out was [dealing with it] mentally," Suggs says, who would rebound to rewrite school, league, and NCAA touchdown records by the time he was finished. "I hardly went to any games. I just wanted to get away from football."

In Suggs' absence, a freshman named Kevin Jones became Tech's rushing leader. Despite not starting until later in the season, Jones finished with 957 yards. Jones was regarded by many as the best recruit in the nation when he signed with Tech, spurning Penn State in the process. He showed up on campus awfully cocky, the polar opposite of the quiet and reserved Suggs. That the two would become friends is proof that opposites attract.

"I knew he was really good. I'd seen him from the all-star games," Suggs says. "I thought he was a little cocky—a whole lot cocky to tell the truth. After a while, you realize that's just Kevin. You have to take him for how he acts. He's a good guy."

They were both good guys, but could they both share the backfield in 2002?

The Setting

What endeared Suggs to those who knew him was the way he handled what happened when he returned from his injury in 2002. He wanted to be the No. 1 back, as did Jones. Hite wanted both of them to be the No. 1 back. Suggs respected Hite's philosophy of not running one back too much, to save

Notes on Lee Suggs

Name:	Lee Ernest Suggs Jr.
Born:	August 11, 1980
Hometown:	Raonoke, Virginia
Current residence:	Roanoke, Virginia
Occupation:	Tailback, Cleveland Browns
Position:	Tailback
Height/Playing weight:	6-0, 202
Years lettered:	1999-2000, 2002
Accomplishments:	Suggs smashed single-season and career touchdown records at Tech in basically two seasons. He was seldom used as a redshirt freshman and played less than three-quarters of a game as a junior thanks to an injury. He scored 28 touchdowns in 2000, doubling the previous school mark. He added 24 touchdowns in 2002. He had 56 career scores, a school and Big East Conference record. Suggs scored at least once in 27 straight games, an NCAA Division I record. He gained 1,207 yards in 2000 and 1,325 in 2002. Suggs is the only two-time winner of The Dudley Award that is given to the collegiate player of the year in the state of Virginia.
Nickname:	TD Lee
The game:	Marshall at Virginia Tech, September 12, 2002

wear and tear. He knew he and Jones could co-exist. After all, their styles were different.

"If we were the same type of backs and the same type of people, we might have clashed," Suggs says. "We got along fine, other than both wanting the same job. We're both competitors. Of course we both wanted to be the man, but we knew for the betterment of the team we needed to share.

"I'm more of a slasher, I try to hit the hole and get up the field. Kevin is a lot more flashy. I remember one game he went over to one side and cut it all the way back to the other. I'd never do that. He's way more daring. He'll risk that, do stuff like running backwards. He'll pay for it sometimes, and it will pay off for him more times. He has the speed to do that."

The school tried to come up with nicknames for the duo, even going so far as conducting a contest. The winner was "The Untouchables," but it didn't stick. Neither did "Thunder and Lightning." They were simply "Lee and Kevin," as good a combination of running backs as a team could hope to have. They would receive a true test against a strong Marshall team that featured quarterback Byron Leftwich.

"Leftwich was getting a lot of publicity as a Heisman candidate," recalls Suggs. "The week before the game, MTV was following him around. There was a lot of talk that they were going to beat us and they were going to throw all over us. There was a lot of talk about our pass defense.

"As usual, we weren't respected enough. We'd beaten LSU in the game before that. For us to beat them and then to come into a Thursday night game against Marshall and not get the respect we deserved, we took that personally."

Game Results

Lee Suggs broke the huddle with a stoic look on his face like he always did. The ball was a yard away from the end zone as the Virginia Tech Hokies looked to complete another drive against the Marshall Thundering Herd. When Tech got inside the 10, it was pretty much automatic that he was going to get the ball and he was going to score. Suggs had what Tech coach Frank Beamer calls "a nose for the end zone."

Quarterback Bryan Randall surveyed the defensive alignment and stepped under center. Having Suggs behind him made Randall's job easier. It

Lee Suggs became a touchdown-scoring machine in a Virginia Tech uniform—setting school, league and NCAA records.

would take something really crazy on the other side of the ball to make Randall change the call. No need this time. He took the snap and turned to hand it off. Everybody in the stadium knew what was coming, especially those in Marshall uniforms.

Suggs let the handoff settle into his stomach. He gripped the ball tight and exploded forward. For Suggs, it was routine: he scored another touchdown.

Suggs and Jones ended up both going over 100 yards in the same game three times that season. Suggs had 197 yards and Jones 132 against Rutgers. Suggs had 154 yards and Jones 144 against Boston College. The Marshall game was the first of the three. Jones had 174 yards and Suggs 153. Each carried 24 times. Suggs played 41 snaps, Jones 35. Jones scored three times, on runs of 25, 15 and 1 yards. Suggs scored twice, both on 1-yard runs in the second half.

That he was outgained by his partner didn't matter to Suggs. That the running game did what it was supposed to do was all that mattered. The Hokies kept the ball away from Leftwich, who put a legitimate scare into them with his passing ability. Tech rushed for 395 yards en route to a 47-21 victory.

"I remember there were about eight minutes left and we're winning by 30-some points and I couldn't relax," Hite says. "Leftwich was just so dangerous. I was afraid they were going to score five times. It was so important to keep the ball away from him and out of their hands."

The Hokies' second drive typified their night. They ran nine plays, all of them featured either Suggs or Jones carrying the ball. Suggs broke off two straight 8-yard runs before Jones went 25 yards to score.

"We ran the same play just about every time, and they couldn't stop either one of them," recalls Bill Roth, the voice of the Hokies. "You could see the Marshall players' heads drop."

Suggs recalls Tech's offensive excellence: "We threw a couple of passes on our first drive. Ernest Wilford had a really nice catch on one of them. As the game went on, we started pounding them. We didn't throw it a lot, and it seems like all of it came in the first quarter.

"Basically, our offense was our defense. We kept Leftwich off the field by running it so much and so well. I know he had a lot of yards in that game,

Suggs had a big day against Marshall, as did teammate and fellow tailback Kevin Jones.

but he got a lot of them in the fourth quarter. It was a very good night for me, a very good night for Kevin, a good night for all of us."

Randall was making the first start of a streak that would grow to 38 by the time he finished. He didn't mind that Tech passed only 11 times.

"We put it down their throats, and I wouldn't trade that for anything," Randall says. "I'll take a 'W' any day."

Even Leftwich left impressed.

"That's what they do," he said after the game. "They don't talk about those guys like that for nothing. We knew they were great players before we got here and they did their jobs. Give those guys credit because they beat us royally."

* * *

For the longest time, it looked as if Suggs and Jones would both go over the 1,000-yard mark for the season. They sent the Tech sports information department scrambling for information on the top totals registered by two backs on the same team. But later in the season, Jones injured a hamstring. He finished the regular season with 836 yards. Suggs ended up with 1,255 yards and won another Dudley Award. He's the only player with two of them.

"Two very unselfish players," Hite says of the pair of backs. "You could hear them when they were coming off the field, always helping each other out. There was never any bitching about not getting the ball enough, not getting enough yards."

Had he wanted, Suggs could have appealed for another year. But he knew his work at Tech was done, and that the position was in good hands with Jones coming back. Suggs headed to the NFL. Meanwhile, Jones set a single-season record in 2003 with 1,647 yards and headed to the NFL himself.

"That two-back thing worked out well my last year," Suggs says. "My whole career worked out well, better than I thought it would when I signed. I'm really glad I made that choice."

So are many others. Quiet and efficient, Suggs was as popular a player as anyone who has ever played at Tech. Fanfare didn't really matter. He just wanted to do his job.

Suggs and teammates celebrate one of Suggs' many touchdowns.

"You had to be impressed with Lee, the way he battled back from that injury and scored all those touchdowns," says Mike Burnop, who now does color commentary on Tech's radio broadcasts.

Roth agrees: "Lee Suggs was the perfect football player. Great kid, great family. You cry when a kid like that gets hurt. He came back better than ever. Lee was an incredible player and a better guy."

CHAPTER 20

BRYAN RANDALL

Bryan Randall left Virginia Tech as one of the Hokies' most honored players of all time. He set a number of records and won a trophy case full of awards. Ask anybody around Tech about Randall, though, and his considerable skills won't be the first thing mentioned. As good a player as he was at Tech, Randall was a much better leader. He had "it," the collection of intangibles that helped him become as respected as he was decorated.

Randall won the 2004 ACC player of the year award in a landslide with stats that were very good. But his leadership on a team that won an ACC championship in its first year in the league is what cinched the deal. He became the face of a team that won the ACC's sportsmanship award as well as its championship.

"You get here, and there's a lot of things you don't know, a lot of things you are nervous about. You don't really know who to talk to," said receiver Eddie Royal, a freshman during Randall's senior season. "I didn't have that problem because Bryan grabbed me as soon as I got here, and he's been my mentor ever since. He's been a great person to look up to, a great role model."

The men's basketball team knew what Royal meant. After Randall's junior football season ended, he joined the basketball team for the final three months of the season. Making the transition from gridiron to hardwood wasn't a stretch. As a junior in high school, Randall was the Virginia basketball player of the year in the AA classification. He had "game."

But his biggest value to the team was his leadership skills. "Bryan is a winning person," Tech basketball coach Seth Greenberg said. The Hokies were playing three freshmen during that season, and Randall's influence was huge.

"He helped us out a lot," said guard Jamon Gordon, who was one of those freshmen. "One game I remember in particular, we played Syracuse and we were down at the half. He gave a speech, he sounded just like Vince Lombardi.

"I learned so much from him, about how to go out there and play hard every day."

Randall thought his stats would have been less meaningful without his leadership ability.

"I believe they go hand in hand," he says. "I believe there aren't that many great leaders. There are a lot of guys who can strap it up and go out there and throw and run. When you're talking about good leaders, they don't come around every day.

"There's something special about that. A lot of times I feel it is taken for granted. A lot of people think a good player is going to be a good leader, which is not true."

The Setting

Randall's leadership may have been his best asset, but he earned respect at Tech for another reason. During his junior season, the Tech coaching staff seemed intent to give the quarterback job to redshirt freshman Marcus Vick. Though Randall started every game, Vick got the bulk of the playing time in several of them. From one week to the next, Randall wasn't sure of his status. It got frustrating at times, yet Randall kept quiet and kept working.

It wouldn't be a problem in Randall's senior season, because Vick was suspended from school after a variety of legal problems. Suddenly Randall was the team's only experienced quarterback.

"It was different," Randall says of his junior season. "That's not what I expected that season to be like, the second part of it anyway. The first part was fine.

"My goal coming back was to make my senior season my best year, knowing it was my last go 'round. I wanted to go out on top. I wanted to go

Notes on Bryan Randall

Name:	Bryan Jemar Randall
Born:	August 16, 1983
Hometown:	Williamsburg, Virginia
Current residence:	Williamsburg, Virginia
Occupation:	On the Atlanta Falcons' preseason roster after spending the 2005 season on the Falcons' practice squad.
Position:	Quarterback
Height/Playing weight:	6-0, 228
Years lettered:	2001-04
Accomplishments:	Randall took over as Tech's starter early in his sophomore season and didn't miss a start the rest of his career. His 38 straight starts are a record for a Hokies quarterback. In 2004, he was the Atlantic Coast Conference player of the year and won the Dudley Award that goes to the player of the year in the state of Virginia. He holds the school records for passing yardage and total offense.
Nickname:	B-Rand
The game:	Virginia Tech at Georgia Tech, October 28, 2004

out with a bang. I wanted to make it to the national championship, if not a BCS bowl. It was something I felt was destined to happen. For some reason, I feel like things have always worked out for the better, one way or another."

Game Results

Before the final five minutes of the Georgia Tech game, it looked like Randall's prognosis might be off. But then Randall's leadership took over, as he showcased over the final moments of the game all of his attributes—his arm, his legs, and his intangibles.

Randall is quick to point out that he had nothing to do with one big play that made the memorable comeback against Georgia Tech more reasonable. The Yellow Jackets were driving for a touchdown that would have put them up by 12 points. Redshirt freshman linebacker Xavier Adibi, playing his first game since the season opener because of an injury, came up with a big sack of Georgia Tech's Reggie Ball that forced the Yellow Jackets to settle for a field goal.

"What a great play by Xavier. We really needed that," Randall says. "If they go in for the touchdown there, it puts a little more pressure on us, and their defense can play a little more relaxed. After they got a field goal, I was thinking we had to go down quick and get a touchdown. I wasn't thinking field goal at all. Time was getting kind of late."

Tech got the ball on the Yellow Jackets' 20. The Hokies called a play action pass, though Randall didn't think anybody would bite on the run at that point. He still thought the play could work. He never expected to find Royal all alone 30 yards downfield.

"The safety ended up biting on a route by the tight end going down the middle. I saw the safety kind of stay with him," Randall recalls. "I looked over at Eddie, he was standing there wide open, waving his arms. I was thinking, 'Do I have enough time to get this off?' If you look at the film, the way I threw the ball was like it was a hot potato. My feet weren't really set. It was kind of a jump pass, very awkward. Without thinking, I just threw it. Eddie made it happen after the catch."

Royal made it happen all the way into the end zone—an 80-yard reception that brought the Hokies to within two points.

Bryan Randall used his leadership skills to help both the football and basketball teams at Virginia Tech.

"As soon as I got by the defensive back, I got real excited because I knew he would see me. After scoring the touchdown he was the first person I saw, and I couldn't wait to celebrate with him," Royal says.

Going for two points was the only choice. Five minutes remained, so there was plenty of time for Tech to get the ball back and score again. But one point was meaningless in that situation and, with so much time left, missing the two wouldn't have been a killer. Getting it would have meant "the momentum would really be on our side. It was crucial," Randall says.

During his career, Randall had been a part of some big plays, but he hadn't yet experienced what *Richmond Times-Dispatch* columnist John Markon called "an Elway moment," bringing a team back from behind the way John Elway did so often in his career. This was his chance, and he thought about it as he walked to the line to run the two-point play.

The call was pretty basic: Randall would take the snap, roll right and look for one of several options for a short pass. If nothing was there, he could try to run it into the end zone. The problem was, Randall had too much company of the wrong variety as he rolled to the right—a crew of Georgia Tech defenders. A glance showed no one open. The defenders drew closer. Still, no one was open. Then, out of the corner of his eye, Randall caught a glimpse of Richard Johnson. He was a decoy on the play, but he was also wide open, albeit a long way away on the other side of the field.

Randall had no choice now. Off balance, he flung it as hard as he could toward Johnson, just as the Yellow Jackets knocked him down. Johnson caught the ball. The game was tied.

It was possibly the best play of Randall's career, one that doesn't even show up in his passing stats. He had the experience to know just how long he had before he had to get rid of the ball. And he had enough arm strength to get it to Johnson even though Randall was not in a position to use perfect passing form.

"I was on my back as soon as I let it go," Randall recalls. "Richard was a decoy, but when I saw nobody open to the right, my first instinct was to look back, and he was wide open. They were about to sack me. My instinct was to jump up and throw it. By the grace of God, I had enough strength to get it over there.

"Those two points were big at the time, very crucial for momentum."

Against Georgia Tech as a senior, Randall passed and ran the Hokies to a fourth-quarter rally.

Virginia Tech's defense forced a quick punt. On the second play of the drive, Randall rushed for 32 yards. On the next play, he hit Josh Morgan for a 51-yard touchdown.

"We'd been having pretty good success in getting to the middle," Randall says. "On that run, the big thing was making one guy miss. When I got to the line I was able to put a move on the middle linebacker, and I knew I was going to be able to make a good run. At that point, I knew nothing was going to stop us. We had them on their heels.

"We knew they liked to bring a corner blitz, and on the next play I saw the safety cheating over. I knew the corner was going to blitz, which meant we had to do an adjustment route. Luckily we were on the same page. The thing that made it special was Jesse Allen, our fullback, was able to get over there and pick up the cornerback. That gave me enough time to see everything, and I was able to get it to Josh."

In the two drives, the Hokies ran four plays and gained 163 total yards. They needed only 1:16 to get them. The Hokies added a touchdown on a Roland Minor interception late in the game to make the final 34-20. They won the rest of their regular-season games, finishing with an eight-game streak before being stopped by unbeaten Auburn in the Sugar Bowl.

A loss in the Georgia Tech game likely would have led to more. As it was, the Hokies won close games over North Carolina and Miami later in the season.

"The Georgia Tech game was the turning point of the season," Randall says. "We were down at halftime, and a lot of people had doubts about whether we'd be able to come back.

"The question had always been big: 'Can Randall bring them back from behind, is he capable of doing that?' We never had doubts. We went in at halftime and knew we were going to do it, we were going to find a way to win."

The halftime session was where the leadership skills of Randall and the team's other seniors became invaluable. Tech coach Frank Beamer said after the game that he didn't have to say anything to his team at the break. By the time he got to the locker room, the seniors had said everything.

"I didn't actually give a talk," Randall says. "I was walking around the locker room, telling everybody to keep their heads up. I was just telling people, 'We're going to get it done.'"

Royal recalls: "He kept us motivated. We were young. When you get down you want to hang your head and get discouraged. He wouldn't let us do that. I remember going into the locker room, everybody was down, thinking the season was going downhill. Bryan and a few of the seniors let us know that wasn't going to happen, that we were the better team and we were going to go out there and make it happen.

"And when it was time to make a play, Bryan made a play for us."

Randall adds: "When we won that game, there was no doubt in our minds [about the rest of the season]. We felt like we were battle tested, that we had the burden off our backs of not being able to win a close game, being able to win when we're down. Once you figure that out, it seems like it was contagious."

It was the high moment in a season full of them, a fine ending for a guy who a year earlier had to fight for his job every week.

"There were some ups and downs over the four years," Randall says. "My senior year was definitely my best.

"It was a very satisfying part of a very satisfying season. To win the ACC championship and win ACC player of the year were great. Coach [Kevin] Rogers told me all the time that if I played the way I was capable of playing, I could win those awards.

"It's funny, people always wondered if I could lead a comeback like that, if we could win the close games. You win a couple, and all of a sudden it becomes, 'He isn't going to let us lose. He can throw the big one now.'

"I've always found ways to win ballgames—one way or another. ... I'm a winner, that's what I do. I'm not saying I'm going to go out and throw it 80 yards or run a 4.1 [second 40-yard dash], but you talk about finding ways to win, that's always been in my resume. I'm going to find ways to win. That's something everybody doesn't have, either."

CHAPTER 21

MIKE IMOH

Mike Imoh has dealt with doubters his entire life. The criticism: too small.

"He's been told that his whole life," says Billy Hite, Tech's assistant head coach and running backs coach. "He's not big enough. He's not fast enough. He's not strong enough."

He was too small to succeed at Robinson High in Fairfax, Virginia, one of the state's best high school programs. All he did was become the player of the year in Group AAA, the highest of three classifications in Virginia. Imoh then headed to Tech, with the memories of people telling him he was making a mistake ringing in his ears.

"From the jump you hear, 'You're too small, you're not fast, you can't make that block,'" Imoh says. "I've always had that—always. That's something that just doesn't go away from me. People said, 'You'll never start at Virginia Tech.' They say I'm a third-down back, I'll get a couple of carries here and there, get a couple of catches. That's not something any back wants to hear.

"When I was putting up big numbers in high school, people were like, 'You're not playing anybody.' Then you get here and people say, 'You're not going to be able to step on the field.' It's been going on forever, and it has always been my motivation. I've never understood why people think a running back has to be tall. It makes no difference. There's only a few positions where height makes a difference. Heck, it's even a bit of an advantage. Tall people seem like they're looking down. Everything is right in front of me. I can also get behind those big linemen and squirt out somewhere else."

At Tech, Imoh faced the same doubters, and just as he had done in high school, he set about proving each and every one of them wrong.

The Setting

Imoh had extra motivation for the 2004 season. He was involved in an offseason incident that ultimately ended with him being suspended for the first three games of the year. It was a crushing development for a young man who had always tried to do the right thing, a young man whose reputation was important to him and well earned. A momentary lapse in judgment threatened that.

The reputation could be repaired, but the three games could not be regained. For a competitor of Imoh's class, it was painful to watch games from the sideline.

"I knew I had to move on from it, that I couldn't stay stuck in the past," Imoh says. "I had to let people know what I'm really all about, and the best way to do that was take care of my business on and off the field. I had to get the fans back behind me, get the coaching staff back to trusting me. You definitely have to learn from something like that. You sometimes don't know what you have until you don't have it any more.

"I remember watching the [season-opening] Southern California game, being played pretty much in my back yard. And I'm sitting up here in Blacksburg. It hurt to sit and watch that, watch them fighting so hard and I couldn't help. They came back battered and bruised and I couldn't help. It was a rough feeling."

Once back on the active roster, Imoh quickly established himself as the Hokies' best back. He had 408 yards in five games before playing North Carolina in an early November game. After the UNC game, he was on track to end up over the 1,000-yard mark. A hamstring injury derailed that quest. In fact, the UNC game was his last big one of the season. He only carried the ball 23 times the rest of the way.

"I didn't accomplish all I wanted to that season. The injury definitely set me back," Imoh says.

Notes on Mike Imoh

Name:	Michael U. Imoh
Born:	July 21, 1984
Hometown:	Fairfax, Virginia
Current residence:	Blacksburg, Virginia
Occupation:	Recent graduate of Virginia Tech
Position:	Tailback
Height/Playing weight:	5-7, 197
Years lettered:	2002-05
Accomplishments:	The state Group AAA player of the year at Robinson High as a senior, Imoh earned playing time as a true freshman at Virginia Tech. Before a hamstring injury slowed his junior season, Imoh was on pace for a 1,000-yard season despite sitting out the first three games because of a suspension. Imoh scored touchdowns on runs, passes, and kick returns during his Tech career.
Nickname:	Flea
The game:	Virginia Tech at North Carolina, November 6, 2004

But luckily for Tech, the injury happened after the North Carolina game. There was nothing setting him back that day.

Game Results

On Tech's first drive of the game against the Tar Heels, it gave the ball to Imoh seven straight times. He responded with 55 yards, and had accumulated more than 100 at halftime. He then added 47 yards on the first carry of the second half.

"I remember that long run right after halftime," says Imoh. "I had just come out of the locker room. I had to get an IV at halftime because I'd lost a lot of water. So I came out after the rest of the team. They pulled the IV, put a band aid on me, and I had to run out for the kickoff return, go straight to the huddle with no warmup.

"So the first play, I broke one and ended up getting caught from behind. That run, it would have been nice to take it to the house. After that, it seemed like it was 7, 10, 8, 12 yards every time … it was that kind of day right there. Everything was working so well, everybody on the offense was doing such a good job."

After the game, Tech coach Frank Beamer had nothing but praise for Imoh: "He's tougher than heck and he makes us a better football team. How many yards he got after contact is where you really measure a back."

Imoh finished the day with two touchdowns. He caught one pass and returned three kickoffs for 48 yards in the Hokies' 27-24 victory at North Carolina. He left the locker room thinking he had 236 yards on 31 carries.

"I was exhausted the whole day, every time I came off the field, but I kept getting my second wind," Imoh recalls. "Boom, you get back out there and do it again. When I get out there, I'm trying to give it everything I've got. If you don't leave that field exhausted, you feel like you've let yourself down. I can't do that. The college experience only comes around once. You don't get another chance to play the game. You have to leave it out there."

After the team returned to Blacksburg, Imoh headed to his apartment for some well-earned rest.

That's when things got interesting.

Mike Imoh used the fact that people thought he was too small as motivation.

* * *

Imoh woke up later than normal Sunday morning, the routine for the day after a football game. He was sore, also the norm, especially following a game in which he had 36 "touches." He had run around and through the Tar Heels much of the previous afternoon.

"I was pretty banged up, like usual," says Imoh, generously listed in the program as being 5 feet, 7 inches, and 197 pounds.

After the game, Imoh took some ribbing from teammates and friends. He was told he'd run for 236 yards. That was five short of the school single-game record that Imoh's buddy Kevin Jones had set the year before in a loss at Pittsburgh. Later that night, Imoh and Jones talked by cell phone. Jones congratulated Imoh on the big day and the victory, while getting in some jabs that he remained the record holder.

"I was like, 'I'll get it later,' and he said, 'Call me back when you do,'" Imoh says.

Imoh got dressed and headed out for the Tech training room to get some treatment. As he was walking in, his cell phone rang. It was Hite on the other end.

"Did you call Jones?" Hite asked him.

"Yep," Imoh replied. "I told him I just missed his record."

"Well," Hite answered, "you need to call him back."

Carter Myers works for his family's Ford dealership by day. On football weekends, he helps the Tech radio crew as a statistician. He's known for his accuracy.

"At halftime, Carter showed me the statistics and said they didn't add up to what he had," says Bill Roth, the longtime radio voice of the Hokies. "Carter's statistics always add up. We said we'd take a look at it later. After the game, we're talking about how Mike just missed the record, and Carter said he thought that's where the stats were off."

When he got home, Myers checked his video recorder. He'd set it to tape the game and he went over it play by play. Sure enough, a carry by Imoh in the second quarter had been credited to Justin Hamilton. Myers called Roth. Early the next morning, while Imoh still slept, Roth went to the video office at Tech and checked it out. Myers was right.

Imoh set a school single-game rushing record against North Carolina but didn't know it until the next day.

Roth alerted Dave Smith and Bryan Johnston in the Tech sports information office. They confirmed the mistake. It wasn't their game, so they couldn't make the change. They called their counterparts at North Carolina, who also confirmed the mistake. They could make the change. And they did.

Imoh really had 243 yards on 32 carries. The record was his.

Imoh reached Jones on the phone and presented him with the news. Jones greeted him with disbelief.

"He was all, 'How can you get it a day later?'" Imoh says with a laugh. "I was like, 'This is crazy.' But it was a nice feeling, too. I had no clue they had missed the run. Later we watched the tape and there it was right there. Jones said it was a conspiracy. He said you couldn't get the record the next day."

Imoh calls the record "the icing on the cake." And he still thinks he should have collected even more yards that day.

"I could have maybe gotten it closer to 300 yards. At least 260 or 270," he says. "I think that's one of the things about me, I'm always so hard on myself. I expect so much out of myself. I still don't think I played as well as I could. Watching the film, I could see where I could have had a few more yards here and there.

"But it is nice to have the record, particularly when you consider all the great backs that have played here. They call this place Running Backs U., so that's quite an accomplishment. I don't know how long [the record] will last. It might stick around a couple of years."

* * *

Hite has been at Tech a long time. He coached Kenny Lewis, who held the record until Jones broke it. He's coached Jones and Imoh. A long line of backs who have played under Hite have gone on to the NFL. He stood there that day at UNC and watched the back that people told him wasn't good enough to play at Tech gain more yards than any of them.

"As the game wore on, the hotter he got," Hite says. "He just kept making plays. He was turning 5-yard plays into 15-yard plays. He just had a remarkable afternoon.

"Mike isn't that big. He is well put together, and the work he puts in every off-season allows him to do those things, to touch the ball 39-40 times a game. I remember calling him about the record and him thinking I was kidding him. I told him, 'We're talking about a great back who had that record—and you broke it.' It shows him what kind of back he is and what he's meant to our program. For a guy who is not supposed to be big enough or fast enough, all he does is set records and help you win a lot of games."

BASKETBALL

CHAPTER 22

CHRIS SMITH

In the 1980s, an outstanding basketball player named Gay Elmore left his home state of West Virginia to play at Virginia Military Institute. Elmore enjoyed quite the career at VMI, scoring 2,420 points to rank among the best ever in the state of Virginia. But his decision to leave was never popular in his home state, and Elmore heard about it every time the Keydets went to play at Marshall, one of their rivals in the Southern Conference.

Elmore was hardly a trendsetter. In the late 1950s and early 1960s, Virginia Tech coach Chuck Noe fielded a team that was loaded with West Virginians. At one point, four started and, depending on the substitution patterns, five sometimes played. One of the starters was Chris Smith, a rugged center from Charleston, West Virginia. He came to Tech for a simple reason: The Hokies offered him the best chance to do what he wanted.

"It was easy," Smith says of his collegiate choice. "I wanted to go someplace else where I could take chemical engineering and play basketball. [Tech] really seemed to care about your education."

Coach Noe spent a lot of time recruiting in West Virginia. The state had two pretty good programs of its own at the time. In fact, West Virginia's Mountaineers, led by Jerry West, played in the 1959 NCAA championship game where it lost to California. Marshall also had a talented team.

"Coach Noe was up there like crazy," Smith recalls. "He recruited three off my [high school] team and one off the team that beat us in the state finals. So here were four first-team all-state players that left West Virginia.

They were absolutely devastated. But they didn't really recruit us much until we'd already signed.

"A whole lot of people in southern West Virginia really liked our team because we had so many West Virginians. Now, up in the Charleston area, they wished we'd gone to West Virginia. There was some talk for a while that if I'd gone there, they would have won that 1959 championship game because I might have been able to handle Darrell Imhoff [California's 6-10 center]. West Virginia's sports publicist was later quoted as saying that wasn't right. He said they would have won two national championships if I'd gone there."

The Setting

Smith wasted little time making an impression at Tech. He had long arms and he could jump, attributes that made him a great rebounder.

"Chris was quite a player," says Lewis Mills, a guard who at one point was the only Virginian in Tech's starting lineup. "He had great instincts to go to the ball. He had a great body, long arms, and wide shoulders. He could jump the second, third, fourth, or fifth time just by hitting the floor and going back up as high as he could on his first jump.

"Most people, if they don't get the rebound in a crowd on the first jump, their second jump is not very high. A lot of them have to gather themselves before they jump again. When Chris hit the floor, he went right back up. Even today if you watch the rebounders, that's what they do. They have to gather themselves before they jump again."

Tech was 11-8 in Smith's first season, not bad for a team that started 1-5. It opened his sophomore season with a victory over Virginia, then went to Marshall, where it lost 78-70.

"We just didn't play very well," Smith says.

Tech knew it would get another chance, although the home game in this series was in Bluefield, West Virginia. That wasn't uncommon in those days. One year while Smith was on the team, Tech played 18 games on the road. "We just could not get people to come to Blacksburg," he says.

Three days before the rematch with Marshall, Smith set a school record that still stands. He had 36 rebounds in a game against Washington and Lee that Tech won 105-24.

Notes on Chris Smith

Name:	Chris Smith
Born:	March 31, 1939
Hometown:	Charleston, West Virginia
Current residence:	Charleston, West Virginia
Occupation:	Smith is retired after a career spent in politics and as a chemical engineer. He was city treasurer in Charleston and ran for mayor in 2003. Smith defeated the incumbent in a primary election, but was beaten in the general election.
Position:	Center
Height/Playing weight:	6-6, 235
Years lettered:	1958-61
Accomplishments:	Smith was a charter member of the Tech Hall of Fame. He "is regarded by many as the greatest basketball player in school history," according to the school's media guide. Smith led the team in scoring his final two years and in rebounding all four years. His lowest per-season average was 11.7 and his highest was 20.4 his sophomore year. Blocked shot stats weren't kept when he played, or he'd be on those lists, too. His career scoring average of 18.6 ranks eighth all-time and his career rebounding average of 17.1 ranks first. Three of the four best single-season rebounding marks at Tech belong to Smith.
The game:	Marshall versus Virginia Tech, January 12, 1959

"They had problems getting there—one of the cars bringing them was involved in a wreck," Smith remembers. "We had to warm up and go back out and warm up again. We finally started playing and they came out and held the ball for five minutes. Coach Noe told us to go to the new zone press we were working on. They were just completely harassed. I think the first half they made one out of 17 shots. That's 16 rebounds, and I got most of them."

Playing Marshall a second time promised to provide a tougher test for Tech. Smith would get another chance to play against Marshall's physical center, Ivan Mielke.

Game Results

The game against Marshall had barely started when Smith felt something painful on the back of his head. Mielke had landed a blow just behind Smith's right ear. Smith kept his cool, a difficult task considering what had happened earlier that same season. Mielke had played a little rough in Tech's earlier loss to Marshall, and Smith didn't retaliate because he knew it was usually the second guy—not the person who initiated the contact—who got caught.

But he didn't have to wait long in the second game to get his revenge. Smith went up and grabbed a rebound and, as he turned, felt his right elbow make contact with Mielke's chest. Mielke hit the floor. Smith knew then he'd have clear sailing inside.

"[Mielke] cleared out of the key after that," Smith says. "He may have been trying to pull me away from the basket. He wasn't a good shooter, so I let him roam outside and I played defense inside. When a Marshall player managed to get inside, I was able to help. I didn't even have to worry about Ivan. That also helped me go harder after rebounds on both ends.

"I made all eight of my shots in the second half, and I think all of them came on offensive rebounds."

Rebounding was Smith's forte, but topping 36 against stiffer competition would prove a mammoth task. Smith didn't quite get there; he had to settle for a "mere" 31 rebounds. He also scored 30 points as Tech avenged its loss with a 93-80 victory. Today, getting a "double-double"—at least 10 points and 10 rebounds—is impressive. Smith became a 30-30 man

Chris Smith was among a number of West Virginians who played basketball at the same time at Virginia Tech.

against Marshall. He's the only Tech player to do that—and he did it twice. Smith had 32 points and 31 rebounds against VMI the following season.

"Marshall was fast, maybe the best running team I had ever seen," says Smith. "They could really get up and down the court. ... We played an unusual defense against them the next time, sort of a man to man with a one-man box. It wasn't a box and one, it was a one-man zone. It was a strange defense, but it worked great. That's how I was able to get a lot of rebounds.

"We really wanted to show Marshall we were better than the last time we'd played them. ... Statistically at least, I had my best game to that point. It was a good night for us."

Having a huge game against Marshall was satisfying for Smith for so many reasons—revenge, the fact that so many family members and friends came to see the game, and because it came against a team from his home state.

Life After Tech

Smith was as serious with his school work as he was on the court. Mills calls him "brilliant," adding, "Chris was one of the best student-athletes you'd ever want to meet. Engineering was a full-time thing, and yet he was able to take care of his school work and play basketball."

By the time he was finished, Smith established numerous other rebounding records that still stand. He had a chance to play pro basketball, both in the NBA and the old ABA. He was drafted by Syracuse with the fifth pick in the second round of the 1961 NBA draft, making him the 14th player picked overall. No other Tech player has been picked higher.

At that time, Smith knew he could make more money putting his engineering degree to work, so that's what he did. Retired now as a chemical engineer and politician, Smith spends time with his family while working on several of his own books. He remembers his Tech career with great fondness and takes tremendous pride in being part of the inaugural class in the Tech Hall of Fame. He was the only basketball player in that class.

Noe, his coach, died in 2003. At the time of Smith's induction, Noe was the host of a weekly radio show in Richmond, Virginia. He went on the air with a tribute to Smith.

His rebounding prowess overshadowed the fact that Smith was a good scorer, too.

"Personal stats—they did not mean a thing to him," Noe said. "All he wanted to do was win. He had tremendous spirit, a heart as big as a football stadium. … Chris Smith was a coach's dream."

Noe's tribute also referred to a conversation between Elgin Baylor and Jerry West. Baylor had to guard Smith in a postseason tournament that included college and pro players. Baylor asked West just who was this Smith guy?

"West, knowing first-hand just how devastating Chris could be, smiled and said, 'I told you he was tough, and if we had recruited him at West Virginia, we would have won two national championships in a row,'" Noe said.

CHAPTER 23

GLEN COMBS

Glen Combs grew up the son of a basketball coach. Morton Combs drilled fundamentals into his son in the small town of Carr Creek, Kentucky, so small "I wouldn't even call it a town," Glen Combs says.

In Kentucky, it didn't matter how small the town. If you could play basketball, they'd find you, and Combs was no exception. The University of Kentucky didn't seem to have much interest, but plenty of other schools did, among them Virginia Tech. Bill Matthews was the head coach at Tech at the time, though he'd be gone by the time Combs enrolled. One of his assistants was Charlie Moir, later a head coach at Tech. Moir took a trip to Kentucky to get a look at Combs.

"A great shooter," Moir recalls. "I saw him in the Kentucky-Indiana all-star game. He played on the same team as Wes Unseld. He had tremendous range on his shot, and he was a very intelligent player. That's what really impressed me about Glen. He was so well coached, he was so fundamentally sound. He could shoot the basketball with the best of them."

Moir got to coach Combs for one year on the freshman team, since freshmen weren't allowed to play varsity basketball then. Howie Shannon was coaching the Tech varsity by the time Combs made the move to that team. The results were impressive: Tech lost its opener to Duke, then won 14 of its next 15 games. The season ended with Tech in the National Invitation Tournament, which was a much bigger deal then than it is now. It was the school's first postseason appearance of any kind.

"That's the first flag flying in Cassell Coliseum now—that NIT flag," Combs says. "I felt good coming into my junior year. I spent the summer in Blacksburg just getting ready. I knew all the guys we had coming back and felt like we had the opportunity to have a good season.

"I didn't think it would be near as good as it turned out to be."

The Setting

In 1966-67, for the third straight season, Tech opened against Duke. Unlike the previous two years, Tech came out of this one a winner, 85-71. Up next was Purdue, which featured sharpshooter Rick Mount.

"Beating Duke blew everybody's minds, including the fans and players," Combs says. "Duke was ranked in the preseason polls, and we upset them in the opening game in Charlotte, North Carolina. That kind of set the stage.

"It was a Friday night when we played them, and Saturday we came back home to play Purdue and Rick Mount. It was the largest crowd ever to see a game at that time at Tech. A lot of that had to do with knocking off Duke the night before. We beat Purdue, too. For a young guy coming out of Eastern Kentucky, that was a pretty exciting way to start my junior year."

The win over Purdue was also convincing, a 79-63 final. The season continued to go well for Tech, which put together a four- and a seven-game win streak. But it stumbled to close the season, going 2-3 and dropping the final regular-season game at Toledo, 90-71. Independents like Tech always lived on the edge when it came to the NCAA Tournament, and the loss could have been damaging to a program hoping for its first NCAA Tournament invitation. The 1967 NCAA field included 23 teams—there weren't any at-large bids then. A team won its conference or it didn't get invited.

But the Hokies did get an invite, and oddly enough, they were given a rematch with Toledo in the first round. That game was played in Lexington, Kentucky, and this time, Tech beat Toledo by six points to advance.

"You have to live in Kentucky to understand the importance of basketball," Combs says. "It's like a religion. Basketball is big; it's like football in Florida. To go play there was exciting. I wanted to go back there and do

Notes on Glen Combs

Name:	Glen Courtney Combs
Born:	October 30, 1946
Hometown:	Carr Creek, Kentucky
Current residence:	Roanoke, Virginia
Occupation:	Combs is a retired food broker. He owned his own company in Roanoke for 25 years. He had a seven-year pro career in the ABA that included a league championship with the Utah Stars in 1971, and a year with the Virginia Squires.
Position:	Guard
Height/Playing weight:	6-2, 180
Years lettered:	1966-68
Accomplishments:	A member of the Tech Hall of Fame, Combs averaged 17.9 points for three varsity seasons. He scored 1,361 points and led the team as a junior and a senior, averaging more than 20 points each season.
Nickname:	The Rifleman
The game:	Virginia Tech versus Indiana, March 17, 1967 in Evanston, Illinois

well, [to show the schools there that didn't recruit me], 'Hey guys, here is what you missed.'

"We won, I had an okay game. I don't remember the number of points. I was probably a little anxious and wanted to do well, probably missed some shots I normally would have knocked down. I remember being relieved that we won and that we had a chance to move on."

The team had six days before it had to play Indiana in Evanston, Illinois, on the campus of Northwestern. The Round of 16 matchup against a respectable basketball program was a big deal for a basketball upstart like Tech.

Game Results

The Hokies needed just two more victories to get to the Final Four, but no one gave them much chance against the Hoosiers. Proving the doubters wrong, Tech and Indiana were knotted up in a 56-56 tie as the clock ticked away, less than nine minutes remaining. It was at that point that Combs took over the game, with his father in the stands to cheer him on.

Combs' shot with 8:50 left broke a tie. He made another with 7:35 to play, and then two more in rapid succession. With 5:03 left, Combs converted on a driving lay-up to give Tech a 68-57 lead. It was his tenth point in a 12-1 Hokies run.

Tech ended up winning 79-70. Combs' final line showed 29 points and four rebounds. Teammate Ken Talley added 16 points and 11 rebounds.

"I was forcing some shots early I shouldn't have taken," says Combs. "As the game evolved, I sort of let the game come to me instead of working outside the offense. I basically settled down and started taking the shots that were there instead of trying to force them.

"[Our] team had five guys who could all run and shoot, all of us between 6 feet, 2 inches and 6 feet, 6 inches. Everybody was a pretty good athlete. Coach Shannon pretty much gave me the green light to shoot. … Once I started showing some patience, the shots started falling.

"I do remember those closing minutes. We had a comfortable lead and we realized we had a chance to do something special."

Combs calls the game a "top moment" in his career, because of the magnitude of the game—in the NCAA Tournament against a Big 10 school.

Virginia Tech ventured into Kentucky to recruit sharpshooter Glen Combs, who was nicknamed "The Rifleman."

"Virginia Tech was not well known in basketball at that time," Combs says. "It gave me exposure. I had aspirations to play pro basketball and [that game enhanced] those chances."

Combs and his dad went out to eat after the game. The next day, Tech would take on Dayton, the winner advancing to the Final Four.

"I remember realizing we were now one game away … all of us were kind of, I guess, awestruck at what might happen," Combs said.

Unfortunately, the next day, Dayton ended Tech's run with a 71-66 victory in overtime. Combs had 16 points against Dayton but missed 16 of his 23 shots.

"I had problems all year long on and off with blisters developing," Combs says. "The next day when I woke up I had some real bad blisters on my feet. I ended up basically playing in a lot of pain [against Datyon].

"I know we had a pretty good lead with 2-3 minutes to go, and Dayton whittled away at that. We turned the ball over some. That was the year they initiated the five-second count. You can't just stand there and dribble indefinitely. I remember we got called on that late."

After the season-ending loss to Dayton, the Tech team kept its spirits up in anticipation of another shot during Combs' senior year.

"I guess the disappointment of not going all the way to the Final Four grew as time went on," says Combs. "At that time, we had five starters back for the next season. I think the thinking was, we got here this year ... we have a chance to get to the Final Four again. It didn't happen. What I learned was you have to seize the opportunity while it is there."

Tech has won two NITs since then and been in the NCAA tournament six more times. But it has yet to win more than one game in any of its subsequent NCAA appearances.

"That whole season my junior year was special," recalls Combs. "Beating Duke to start the year, being ranked in the top 20 at one point, beating Indiana in the NCAA tournament. People in Roanoke still to this day remember that game. It was special. It gave me the confidence that I could play against pretty much anybody in college basketball."

Life After Tech

Nowadays, Combs doesn't live too far away from the Tech campus. He's become more involved with the basketball program since Seth Greenberg took over as coach in 2003. He hopes it isn't long before another Tech team puts itself on the edge of the Final Four.

"Coach Greenberg is really making an attempt to reach out to all the former players," Combs says. "I feel like our program is heading back in the right direction. He's an excellent motivator and recruiter. The enthusiasm

Combs' big game against Indiana led Virginia Tech into the final eight of the NCAA tournament.

from the student body had dwindled, and now that's come back. I think Tech basketball is primed to make a positive move."

CHAPTER 24

BOBBY STEVENS

Bobby Stevens was determined to become a Division I basketball player, a desire few others believed was realistic. He was short at 5 feet, 10 inches, and that was the reason for concern.

"I've always had a lot of confidence," Stevens says. "My dad Joe taught me how to lift weights properly. I was fortunate enough to be one of the younger players who lifted weights before it became popular.

"Dad always pushed me to be the best I could be. My mother Thelma was always very competitive. We had a very competitive family, whether it was playing Pinochle, Uno, spoons, horseshoes, ping pong. ... Neighbors would call my folks and say, 'Don't you think your kids should come in?' It was midnight and we were out there shooting baskets. Or we were in the garage playing ping pong—all of us. Even today, I still have that drive."

Offers to play collegiate basketball didn't pour in. One coach suggested he try to go to a prep school first, so he went to Frederick Military Academy.

"After that year, I still didn't have any Division I offers," Stevens says. "Lefty Driesell at Davidson had shown some interest. He had talked about [me] playing my first year there, and I just didn't want to do that. Then Marty Morris, who had been the freshman coach at Richmond and had been recruiting me, got the Ferrum (Junior College) job."

Stevens jumped at the offer.

"There was still an opportunity in two years I could go to a Division I school," he says. "We had two great years. We went to the nationals my freshman year and lost in the first round. My sophomore year, we played for the junior college national championship."

Now he was getting the Division I interest he wanted. Ferrum is not that far from Virginia Tech, and the Hokies were very interested in Ferrum's Charlie Thomas. Tech coach Don DeVoe came to see Thomas one night "and I happened to have a big game," Stevens says. DeVoe ended up signing both players.

"I questioned whether he was big enough to play at Tech," remembers Charlie Moir, then a future Tech head coach who was at Roanoke College while Stevens was at Ferrum. "But he sure proved that he was good enough. He was a competitor. He played to win. He probably excelled on defense more than anything."

The Setting

Playing at the Division I level proved to be the wonderland Stevens dreamed it would be. Among his teammates that first year was Allan Bristow, who scored 1,804 points at Tech before enjoying a long career as a professional.

"The thing about Allan, if he wasn't open you just had to bide your time. He was going to get open," Stevens says. "He was constantly moving. He was 6 feet, 7 inches, but he was our center, and he was generally matched up with a center. If you were going to guard Allan Bristow, you were going to have to run.

"Allan made it so much fun because of his enthusiasm and leadership. He was easy to follow. He always played hard. … The day after we got back from the NIT, he was out back running hills. He said he was getting ready for the NBA draft. That's the kind of guy he was. I don't think he gets enough credit for his leadership for that year. If you look at the next year when I was a senior, we basically had the same team coming back except for Allan and John Payne and we were 13-13."

Bristow enjoyed having Stevens around as much as Stevens enjoyed playing with Bristow.

"To this day, I don't think you'll find anybody more knowledgeable about sports in general. Bobby loves sports, loves talking about sports," Bristow says. "He was a little, spunky point guard, a great dribbler. He was

Notes on Bobby Stevens

Name:	Robert Joseph Stevens
Born:	May 2, 1951
Hometown:	Chester, Pennsylvania
Current residence:	Rock Hill, South Carolina
Occupation:	Science teacher and head boys basketball coach at Rock Hill High School.
Position:	Guard
Height/Playing weight:	5-10, no weight given
Years lettered:	1973-74
Accomplishments:	Stevens was not a star at Virginia Tech, but he played two seasons in a supporting role alongside such standouts as Allan Bristow and Craig Lieder. During the 1972-73 season, Stevens averaged 9.5 points, well behind Bristow's 23.8 and Lieder's 16.1. Assists were not an official stat then. If they were, then Stevens would show up on more of the Hokies' all-time and season leader lists.
The game:	Virginia Tech versus Notre Dame in the NIT final, March 25, 1973

a scrappy player. He could set up the offense and he could get it into the paint. He was very fundamentally sound. He was a great teammate as far as off the court, too."

In 1972-73, Tech went 18-5 in the regular season, winning at Ohio State, Wake Forest, and West Virginia, among other places. That earned the Hokies a spot in the NIT. These days, the NIT isn't as well regarded, commonly referred to as the Nobody's Interested Tournament. But that wasn't the case back in the early '70s.

"It's getting to the point where the younger generation has no clue what the NIT is all about," Stevens says. "It's amazing how many in my generation still remember it from when we played. It gives me a great deal of pride that the alumni are able to talk about such a great event. Even Coach [Bobby] Knight used to talk about the NIT being special. I really think the NCAA tried to water down the NIT field by expanding their field."

Tech escaped the first round of the 1973 NIT Tournament with a narrow 65-63 win over New Mexico. Round 2 proved to be no easier, as the Hokies dispatched Fairfield by a single point. Alabama awaited in Round 3, a game that was also decided by one point, 74-73. Everything seemed to be going Tech's way heading into a matchup with Notre Dame for the tournament championship.

Game Results

If Tech didn't have enough tension to last a lifetime during its first three NIT games, it received plenty more in the final. Stevens had time to soak up the tension, as he spent more time than usual watching the game from the bench. Unhappy with Stevens' play in the first half, DeVoe pulled him.

"I would have taken myself out earlier if I were Coach DeVoe," Stevens says. "We had a 10-, 12-point lead, and I threw it away two or three times. Boom, boom, boom. I took the swing and the momentum from us and put it right back in Notre Dame's lap. I had a tendency to turn around and foul right away in my excitement to try and get it back.

"Don was right. That's coaching, knowing your players. He brought me out to let me sit there and see things."

Tech trailed the Irish by 12 with a little more than six minutes to play. Stevens came off the bench to help bring the Hokies back. He had three late

After missing moments earlier, Bobby Stevens drilled the shot to beat Notre Dame in overtime in the final of the 1973 NIT.

baskets and then assisted on a basket by Craig Lieder that tied the game and forced overtime.

Notre Dame took a one-point lead late in overtime when Dwight Clay made a foul shot. He missed the second. Tech took possession, got to halfcourt, and called timeout. Coming out of the time out, Stevens raced the ball downcourt to set up a final play. The Hokies had three options. The first was to look for Bristow; the next was to go to Lieder, another proven scorer; and the third option was for Stevens to shoot.

"Problem was, he did the third option first," Bristow recalls.

Stevens let the shot go from the top of the key, just to the right of the circle. It missed and kicked off at a 45-degree angle away from Stevens. He didn't hesitate chasing the ball down. This time there was no option—no time to think or look. All Stevens could do was shoot it again.

"I always kid people that I grabbed the rebound and threw it back out to him," Bristow says with a laugh. "That really ticks him off. He did run it down. He didn't have time to think about it then. But he got off a good shot."

Time seemed to freeze. Stevens recalls watching Lieder raise his arms early as if he knew it was going to fall. Lieder was right. The shot went in, giving Stevens seven points in the overtime period and 17 for the game. Most important, it gave the Hokies a 92-91 victory and the NIT title.

"What a great feeling," Stevens says. "Even as I watch it today, I'm waiting for that shot to miss. ... It was a great feeling, and 32 years later I still get excited about it. It's something you're always trying to obtain—some kind of national title. I was fortunate enough to be with some good people and we just put it all together.

"We didn't get to bed until late and I suddenly just woke up. I had this rush of, 'We won the NIT!'"

Bristow remembers Stevens having something of a delayed reaction to the winning shot. It didn't last long, as he was soon on the shoulders of his teammates.

"If you look at the picture right after, Craig and I have our hands up in the air like, 'Hey, we won,'" says Bristow. "Bobby was still sort of frozen from that shot. Then it was, 'Oh, yeah, we won the NIT.'"

Every game was a cliffhanger for Tech during the '73 NIT. Bristow notes that Tech's refusal to lose displayed "the resiliency of that team."

Stevens enjoys the ride after his buzzer-beating shot gave Virginia Tech the 1973 NIT championship.

Stevens agrees: "I really think it proved the type of team we had. We weren't a totally talented team that just blew people out. It was almost like the games we played in, those were the types of games we expected to play for the fans. No one wants to go to the concession stands, take a restroom break, until the game is over.

"When you look at [that 1973 team], Allan was a superstar of that era. A great scorer, great hands, great athlete. ... I wish every point guard had the opportunity to play with a guy like that. ... You'd get it within three or four feet of his arm span and he'd catch the ball. He was the John Havlicek of his day.

"From that point down [the roster], I don't know if you could say there were any super athletes. What made us so good was the chemistry. Everybody understood their role. I was a scoring point guard. When I got to Tech, Don [DeVoe] didn't want me shooting the ball. He wanted me running the offense and putting pressure on the ball. He turned Charlie Thomas into a defender. Craig Lieder would take a charge on a locomotive if he had to. We had a mix and a blend of people who came off the bench. Dave Sensibaugh was a little bit of a scorer and a pusher. Everybody understood their role.

Stevens and his teammates earned the NIT trophy by winning a series of close games including one in overtime against Notre Dame in the final.

"We weren't talented like some of the teams today. We were hard-nosed kids who understood how to play. We complemented one another and truly liked each other. ... It was truly a family of sorts."

Reflecting on Tech

Stevens spent a long time as a collegiate coach—including time spent as an assistant at Tech—before going to the high school ranks. When the coaching staff's contracts were not renewed at Winthrop College, Stevens opted to stay in the area, because his daughter, who played volleyball and softball, was in high school then and he didn't want to move his family again. So Stevens converted to coaching at the high school level. He misses the talent level of the collegiate game, but enjoys coaching on any level almost as much as he enjoys being reminded of his big shot in Madison Square Garden that gave the Hokies their first NIT title.

"It was really something special," he says. "There were a lot of people involved in that, and it's brought a lot of joy to my life. A lot of doors and opportunities opened for me because of that. People want to talk about it, just talk about that moment. I wish I had a nickel for every time somebody tells me, 'I was at that game,' or where they were and who they were with and the damage they did when they jumped up on the coffee table. It brought a lot of joy to a lot of people.

"I don't think I really understood the magnitude of it at that time. ... One of the things that gave me the biggest pleasure was after the game there was this kid just pounding on my back. It was my little brother Jim, who would have been 16 at the time. How he got out of the stands is beyond me.

"You look at all the thousands and thousands of players who have played and never won a championship. ... If you get that one opportunity to play for a title at any level, you're blessed and fortunate. People ask if I played in the pros. I tried out for the Virginia Squires. I wasn't good enough. But even the greatest players don't always get to experience what I experienced."

CHAPTER 25

LES HENSON

Les Henson liked Don DeVoe. That's why he decided to play basketball at Virginia Tech, so he could play for Coach DeVoe. But before he ever got to Tech, the school fired DeVoe and replaced him with Charlie Moir. DeVoe told Henson to follow him to Wyoming, where the coach would treat him like a son, according to Henson.

"I'm sure he would have," Henson says, "but I wasn't going to Wyoming. Tech had always shown the most interest in me. I went to a game where Tech played at the University of Richmond and, man, it seemed like three-quarters of the people there were Virginia Tech people. I'm thinking, 'Man, they really follow their sports at Tech.' That's when I really made up my mind to go there.

"After Coach DeVoe got fired, Coach Moir came to get me to sign, and I told him I didn't feel comfortable signing with somebody I didn't even know. So I didn't. I got to know him a little better and then signed. He struck me as someone a lot like my high school coach, Warren Rutledge. He was the best I ever had as far as knowledge and temperament and all that. Coach Moir seemed to have that. He was low key and had a good sense of humor. I signed and it ended up being pretty good."

It ended up being really darn good. Tech had excellent records each of Henson's four seasons in uniform, playing in postseason three times including the NCAA tournament twice. In Henson's junior year, Tech lost in the NCAA Tournament to Indiana State and Larry Bird.

"I remember most everything about that game," Henson says. "I remember Larry Bird was more of a passer than a shooter. He didn't really do anything against us that was phenomenal. They ended up going to the national championship game. They must have done something right."

The Setting

Henson was a fixture in the Hokies' lineup his entire career, though he was never the team's star. He could do a little bit of everything. Some nights he'd rebound, some nights he'd score, some nights he'd do both—and then some. He was exactly the type of player a winning team needs—a guy below the star line who is pretty darn good.

"I was just a good all-around player," Henson says. "The way I was taught to play the game, you try to win as a team. You don't try to score a lot of points. I thought a strong part of my game was that I was a real good passer. I'd help rebound. I led the league in free throw shooting as a junior.

"All those kinds of things, the dirty work things that always seemed to go unnoticed until a guy like Dennis Rodman came along."

Adds Moir: "Les ... was certainly one of the top athletes and one of the top players I coached there. It was a pleasure to coach someone who worked as hard as he did to be a good player. He became a fairly good shooter because he worked so hard at it. He made a lot of big plays."

None bigger than a play against Florida State that Henson calls "a fluke."

Game Results

Time was running out in Virginia Tech's Metro Conference basketball game at Florida State. The game had been tied for what seemed like forever. Florida State's Parnell Tookes scored with 59 seconds left to make it 77-77. Tech had an opportunity to go ahead at the foul line with 31 seconds left, but Jeff Schneider missed.

Florida State worked to get the final shot. They went to the 6-9 Tookes again, and he got off a shot from near the foul line with about five seconds left.

Notes on Les Henson

Name:	Leslie Henson Jr.
Born:	July 10, 1957
Hometown:	Richmond, Virginia
Current residence:	Raleigh, North Carolina
Occupation:	Developer of apartment complexes. Henson has had a variety of jobs in the sales field.
Position:	Forward
Height/Playing weight:	6-6, 190
Years lettered:	1976-80
Accomplishments:	Henson was one of the hidden stars on a series of very good Tech basketball teams. Overshadowed by stars such as Duke Thorpe, Wayne Robinson, and Dale Solomon, Henson scored 1,334 points during his career. He's among Tech's leaders in field goal percentage for a career (51.7 percent), and twice led the team in free throw shooting percentage.
The game:	Virginia Tech at Florida State, January 21, 1980

"I could tell right away it wasn't even close to going in," Henson recalls. "You could tell that from the flight of the ball. It hit the side of the rim and kicked off into the corner. I ran into the corner and got it. People tell me to this day my foot was out of bounds. I say it was not, it was just the camera angle.

"I got it and turned around. Dexter Reid was at halfcourt, yelling at me to get it to him. I knew we didn't have time for that. So I just turned around and threw it. [Then] everything seemed to slow down."

Henson, a lefty, heaved the ball with his right hand. A measurement taken later showed he was 89 feet, 3 inches away from the basket. The crowd at FSU's Tully Gym got quiet as the ball cut through the air … and swished.

"It's going up and I thought, 'It is going to hit the rafters,'" Henson says. "They had a flag hanging down, and I thought it was going to hit that. Then I thought, 'No, that thing has a chance.'

"The thing about it was, it just went in clean. It didn't hit the back of the backboard or anything. It went in clean as a whistle. As it was approaching, everything seemed to just stop. Even on the audio, it sounds like the wind has gone out of the place. Nobody could believe it.

"I just turned around and said to one guy nearby, 'Can you believe that?' Dale Solomon caught up with me and picked me up and ran down the hall with me. Everybody was going, 'What in the world?'"

Moir's first reaction was to check with the officials to make sure the shot counted. Assured that it did, he jumped as high as humanly possible. His counterpart, FSU's Joe Williams, was a good friend, and the two had a sandwich together after the game. Right after the shot dropped, Williams was not in much of a celebratory mood.

"It's the most incredible thing I've ever seen," Williams told reporters afterward. "Henson hitting that miracle shot is like a golfer winning a tournament with a 100-foot putt over three mounds and two gulleys."

Memphis State coach Dana Kirk was at the game scouting, which was legal in those days.

"If I had been the coach and someone had done that to me, I would start checking how many years I had left on my contract," he told reporters.

More than a quarter of a century later, Moir remains amazed.

Les Henson did a little of everything for Virginia Tech's basketball team.

"It was a thrill, it really was. It was a shock," Moir says. "What a great moment. I didn't anticipate it getting anywhere near the basket. I remember thinking, 'My God, my God, it went in!'"

Henson scored 20 points that night, missing only three of 11 shots. Yet people only seem to remember two of those points—the two that gave the Hokies a 79-77 win. He became something of an instant celebrity. Cable television highlights were a relatively new thing in those days, and that shot was shown over and over again.

"I've always considered it lucky," Henson says. "It was a once-in-a-lifetime thing.

"At this point right now, people don't remember me, per se. They don't remember me as a ballplayer. They remember that shot. People called me from the Virginia Tech booster club. They said people only asked them about a few people, where are they now kind of thing. One of them was Kylene Barker, who went on to become Miss America. One of them was me."

For a while, Henson says, it bothered him that people didn't remember anything other than his long shot. Eventually, he came to understand that it could be a lot worse.

"I wouldn't say it was resentment," he says. "I would say it was more disappointment that people didn't see me as more than a guy who made a long shot. Now that I've gotten older, I know that it was a blessing to play at that level, to see what I saw, to be around the people I was around. I have lifelong friends from playing. I'm still in touch with a lot of those guys.

"For every Michael Jordan and Kobe Bryant, for every superstar, there are a lot more guys like me who are pretty good but didn't really get a lot of recognition. At the same time, I feel like I was lucky to be there. Basketball took me places I wouldn't have normally been."

Life After Tech

Henson has yet to live down "the shot."

"Every time someone hits a long shot these days, I know people are going to call. It happens every time," he says. "Just today, I ran into a guy and we were talking. He asked me my name. I'm older, I've gained a lot of weight, and I'm down here in North Carolina. He said, 'I remember that

Every time someone hits a long game-winner, Henson receives phone calls asking him about his long shot that beat Florida State.

name.' It's totally weird how people remember things, especially in sporting events. I'm still flabbergasted by it.

"People wanted me to try and recreate the shot, too. Later in my senior year, I got letters from this agent who would pay me to go around to places and try to recreate the shot. I told him I was interested, but not right then. It never really materialized."

Henson hasn't been back to Tech, he says, in nearly 20 years. The basketball regime has changed several times over, and he doesn't really know anybody in the department anymore. But they know him. Newspaper pages detailing his shot are on the walls of the school's athletic department. It was quick and it was lucky, but it still ranks as one of the school's greatest moments.

"It's funny the way things work," Henson says. "I remember reading a story where Len Elmore and Dick Vitale were walking through an airport and Len walked up to a guy and they were hugging and talking and Dick goes, 'Who is that?'

"It was David Thompson. He was the greatest college player ever and people don't remember him. He won a national championship.

"A guy like me? I'm lucky to be remembered at all."

CHAPTER 26

DELL CURRY

Whenever Dell Curry hears the Bruce Springsteen song "Glory Days," the line about throwing that speedball by you has to bring a smile to his face. Curry could throw that speedball by you, make you look like a fool. He made his fame and fortune playing basketball, but it was not his favorite sport. Curry was a good enough pitcher that he was drafted by the Major Leagues on two occasions—once out of high school and once while at Virginia Tech on a basketball scholarship.

"I liked baseball better than basketball," Curry says. "In high school, my dad turned [the Major League contract] down for me. He said, 'Son, you're going to college.' That decision wasn't hard at all. When the Orioles drafted me while I was in college, I thought about it for a while. They wanted to give me a decent bonus, and I thought about it before going back to school.

"A lot of people thought I was better in baseball than basketball. If I'd gone that way, hopefully I wouldn't be sitting here now. I'd still be pitching at 41 in the big leagues. If I could have had any guarantee I would have made it to the big leagues, I would have played baseball."

Curry only pitched one season at Tech. As a junior, he posted a 6-1 record. The one loss came when he made a throwing error after fielding a bunt. "He was aiming at some University of Virginia fan's car," says longtime Hokies baseball coach Chuck Hartman.

He wasn't just a guy the Hokies threw out there against overmatched teams. Curry won against South Carolina and Florida State on the road.

"He could have pitched professionally, might have even pitched in the big leagues," Hartman says. "He had big, long arms, a good curveball, and he had enough pop on it. He was throwing 87-89 miles per hour, and he'd been out of baseball a couple of years before he joined us.

"He wasn't out there to get fans in, he was very legitimate. He was such a good athlete. He had a nice loose arm, almost like a bullwhip. He snapped it when he threw it. God just gave him some unbelievable athletic ability. Plus, he was a great guy. Our baseball guys loved him."

Charlie Moir, Tech's basketball coach when Curry played there, knew he was recruiting an excellent pitcher.

"I saw him pitch a state playoff game where they won," Moir recalls. "He could fire that baseball. He had all the ingredients to go all the way in baseball. He could throw it hard, and he had big ol' strong wrists."

Basketball just happened to be the sport that worked out for Curry, and even Hartman agrees, "Dell made a good decision in life. He's done well."

The Setting

In each of Curry's four years at Tech, the basketball team went to postseason play. Tech doesn't have as rich and deep a basketball tradition as a lot of schools. It has had its moments and a number of good players. Ask enough people who the best of the bunch was, and most will say Curry.

Curry is No. 2 on the school's all-time scoring list. That deserves a closer look. He's 95 points behind Bimbo Coles, an excellent player who came in the year Curry left and, like Curry, went on to enjoy a long career in the NBA. He had one game at Tech where he scored 51 points and handed out 11 assists. But Coles made 149 baskets from three-point range. Curry made four. The three-pointer didn't become a regular part of the game until after Curry left. His few attempts came during his junior year in games where it was used on an experimental basis.

Had Curry been able to shoot three-pointers his entire career, his point total would be significantly higher. He could shoot from long range. In 1999, he led the NBA in three-point shooting with a 47.6 percent success rate. His NBA career three-point percentage was 40.2.

"Curry was the best player I ever saw at Virginia Tech," says John Markon, a columnist for the *Richmond Times-Dispatch* who has covered

Notes on Dell Curry

Name:	Wardell Stephen "Dell" Curry
Born:	June 26, 1964
Hometown:	Grottoes, Virginia
Current residence:	Charlotte, North Carolina
Occupation:	After a 16-year playing career in the NBA, Curry has settled into the management side of the league. He's director of player development for the Charlotte Bobcats.
Position:	Guard
Height/Playing weight:	6-5, 205
Years lettered:	1983-86
Accomplishments:	Curry is the first men's basketball player at Virginia Tech to have his jersey retired, and he's a member of the school's Hall of Fame as well as the state of Virginia Sports Hall of Fame. He was a three-time all-Metro Conference choice and the league's player of the year as a senior, when he averaged 24.1 points. Curry scored 2,389 points at Tech, the second most ever, and he did it without the three-point shot. His 1,021 career field goals are a school record, and he also holds the school record with 295 steals. Curry was a first-round draft pick of the Utah Jazz in the 1986 draft.
The game:	Memphis State at Virginia Tech, February 1, 1986

college basketball for more than 30 years. "He was a wonderful shooter, every bit as good as someone like J.J. Redick. Curry was reasonable on defense and had good court intelligence. For an alleged 'gunner,' he took very few bad or selfish shots. Remember, he never had the three-point basket to inflate his stats. Most of Curry's jumpers were well behind the current three-point line."

Moir adds: "I remember Dell's senior year we played Michigan in Maui to open our season when Michigan was ranked No. 1. [Tech lost the game, 67-66.] Dell was making shots from the third row of the stands. He was just outstanding. Bill Frieder was coaching Michigan then, and Dell was shooting so well that Bill just looked over at me and threw his hands up.

"We set up a lot of stuff for Dell and he'd work to get himself open, too. He'd come off a screen and he had a tremendously quick release. He shot the ball about as well as anybody."

A couple of weeks before Tech was scheduled to play Memphis State twice in five days during Curry's senior year, the Hokies played a double overtime game at Cincinnati. Curry had a career-high 41 points. Only seven Tech players have ever scored as many as 40 in a game. It says a lot about Curry that he didn't see that game as the game of his life in a Tech uniform. The Hokies lost to Cincinnati by three.

The game against Memphis State meant more to the team than it did to Curry individually, and that's why it meant more to him personally.

"We lost to [Memphis State] earlier," Curry says. "We wanted to come out and show we were better than that."

Quick turnarounds were not uncommon in the Metro Conference. Memphis State—who are now known as the University of Memphis— defeated Tech 83-61 in Memphis. Tech then defeated Richmond three days later in a game in which Curry scored 28 points, only to face Memphis State again in two days, this time at home. Memphis State came to Cassell Coliseum knowing it would rise to number one in the polls with a victory over the Hokies. Just two days earlier, Virginia had knocked off the top-ranked team in the country, North Carolina, creating an opening at the top of the polls.

"Even though Memphis State wasn't really No. 1, in our minds they were No. 1 that night," says Curry. "In their minds they were No. 1—they knew they were going to be if they came in and won against us."

Though he made his mark as a basketball player, Dell Curry was also an accomplished baseball player who probably could have made it to the major leagues.

The Tigers had plenty of weapons, but Tech was no slouch, with a national ranking of 16 at the time. It was a huge game for a Tech team that had lost just four times all season—twice in overtime.

To add to that, Curry was motivated for personal reasons. He had read in a newspaper where Memphis State player Dwight Boyd had called him "lazy" in the aftermath of the Tigers' easy victory over the Hokies. That quote was taped to the wall of the Hokies locker room, serving as additional motivation. As for Curry, he wasn't a big talker then, and he isn't a big talker now. Brash joins lazy on the list of things Curry is not. He figured he'd keep his mouth shut and give his answer on the Hokies' court when Memphis came to visit.

Game Results

With just over three minutes to play, the Hokies were clinging to a four-point lead. It had been 10 not that long ago, and they were trying to survive the Tigers' run.

"Memphis was awfully talented, and we knew we'd have to play an outstanding game to beat them," Moir recalls. "Someone had to step up, and Dell did. We had to play near perfection."

Curry took a pass and squared up. He was not close to the basket. It didn't matter. His range was pretty much anywhere in the arena. Curry nailed the shot, stretching Tech's lead to six. For Curry, it was just another huge shot in a game full of huge shots. He ended up with another 28-point showing, making 10 of 19 shots from the floor and 8 of 10 from the foul line. He also pulled down nine rebounds, helping Tech to a 42-31 rebounding edge.

Curry had lots of help. Keith Colbert had 16 points and 11 rebounds; Bobby Beecher added 10 points and 13 rebounds; and Roy Brow, a talented sophomore center, hit a late jumper after Memphis State had cut Tech's lead to two. Later, Johnny Fort hit three of four foul shots to keep Tech ahead.

When the buzzer sounded, Tech walked off the court with a 76-72 victory, one that went a long way toward getting the Hokies into the NCAA tournament. Tech fans were appreciative after the game. The *Hokie Huddler* newspaper wrote, "The place didn't go berserk. It just stayed that way."

Curry did most of his damage from long range, but he wasn't afraid to go inside and mix it up against the likes of Memphis State.

Curry and teammates went back out to the court to celebrate with the fans after they'd conducted a team meeting.

"That was great to see them still out there that long after the game," Curry says. "I remember Cassell Coliseum just being electric, even before the game. Students were camping out, getting tickets. It was just an electric atmosphere from start to finish."

"We had tremendous support," Moir says. "We had to come back out for an encore."

This was not the first time Curry and Tech had beaten a well-regarded Memphis State team. As a freshman, Curry was part of a team that beat Memphis after it had risen to No. 1 in the polls. By the time the poll was released in the next morning's newspapers, the Hokies had already toppled them.

The victory over the Tigers in Curry's senior year "gave them the best win in the Curry, Colbert, and Beecher era," the *Hokie Huddler* wrote. "The general consensus in the locker room after the game gave this the nod over a 1983 win over Memphis State when they were No. 1."

"On paper, you'd probably say we had no chance of winning that game," says Curry. "Memphis State had an awfully strong group. On paper, we shouldn't have been in the game. They'd beaten us pretty good less than a week before. Just the fact that we stood up to the challenge is what made that a great night for us."

Moir considers Curry one of the best people he's coached, as well as one of the best players. It doesn't surprise him that Curry turned his nose at higher scoring games in favor of one that meant so much to his team.

"Dell was a worker and a wonderful person to coach," Moir says. "If he had a bad game, you didn't have to tell him to do something extra. He'd be in the gym the next day working. He'd be out there working on his shooting, on his release. He was very dedicated."

Life After Tech

Curry was recently honored as one of the Atlantic Coast Conference's basketball legends, a bit ironic since he never actually played in the ACC. He did consider it, growing up an ACC fan as he did. All the ACC schools

Curry was a scorer who was able to handle himself on the defensive end of the court, too.

showed interest in Curry. Virginia Tech, he thought, was "a better fit for me." A lot of that had to do with Moir, with whom he's still in touch regularly.

"If he was still there, I'd go back there in a heartbeat," Curry says.

Ten of his professional years were spent in Charlotte, and Curry enjoys his current job working with players for the new Charlotte NBA franchise. Curry's professional career lasted about 12 years longer than he expected, and his long pro tenure has earned him a measure of respect that helps as he works with the young Bobcats.

"I help them while they're in the league, and help prepare them for [life] after the league," says Curry, whose oldest son is headed to Davidson University on a basketball scholarship.

"I do a lot of work without words. I hang around them a lot. They watch how a professional carries himself on and off the court. Hopefully they try to imitate that."

CHAPTER 27

CARLOS DIXON

Carlos Dixon was like every other basketball-playing kid who grew up in North Carolina. The ACC was "it," *the* place for college basketball.

"The ACC was basically what kept me interested in basketball," says Dixon via e-mail from China, where he now plays for the Jiangsu Dragons. "There was a game on every day during the basketball season it seemed like. I wasn't a big fan of any of the in-state schools. I usually cheered for Florida State during the Charlie Ward and Bob Sura era. I don't really know why, but I did."

Dixon played just two years at South Rowan High. He made them count. He averaged 18.5 points and 9.3 rebounds as a senior. He was the second leading scorer in school history and was chosen to play in the state's East-West all-star game.

Recruiting interest from ACC schools? None. He went to Fork Union Military Academy for a postgraduate year and got a little bit of interest from Clemson and Wake Forest. He received more from Virginia Tech, which was making the move from the Atlantic 10 to the Big East Conference. It wasn't the ACC, and he wouldn't get to play much in his home state, but the Big East was a big-time league. So Dixon became a Hokie.

The Setting

From Game 1 in a Tech uniform, Dixon was a starter and a major contributor. He was a quality outside shooter, though the first to admit that his shot selection wasn't always great. He was quick enough to drive by a defender if need be, and rugged enough to go inside and battle.

Despite Dixon's talent, the team wasn't very good. During his first three seasons, Tech never even qualified for the Big East Tournament. All a team had to do to qualify was not finish last in its division. Prospects didn't look good for the following year either.

Before that year got started, several things happened. Dixon, who had been bothered by foot problems off and on, suffered a broken bone in his left foot during the off-season. The injury required surgery to fix. Then Ricky Stokes was fired as the Hokies' coach and replaced by Seth Greenberg. Finally, Tech was accepted for membership into the ACC.

The injury and coaching change were difficult times for Dixon. He didn't know how quickly or how well he'd recover. He also didn't know how well he'd fit in with Greenberg and his system. A crew of talented freshmen was joining the program. Would there be room for a senior holdover from the previous staff?

The news of the move to the ACC changed everything. Dixon had been contemplating sitting out a season to make sure he was fully recovered. Now by doing so, he'd finally get a chance to play in the ACC.

"That was a great feeling," he says, "just knowing I would be getting a chance to play against some of the schools that I had been watching all of my life, and for people back at home to finally get a chance to see a local person play on TV.

"It was tough watching the guys play the year I had to sit out, but I knew it would all work out in the end."

Tech did amazingly well the year Dixon sat out. The three freshmen— Zabian Dowdell, Jamon Gordon, and Coleman Collins—were all standouts. Bryant Matthews, the team's lone senior, made the all-Big East team. The Hokies, picked to finish last in the Big East (the league went away from the two division setup), instead finished eighth and got to go to New York for the tournament, where they won a game.

With Matthews gone in 2004-05, Dixon had a place to step right in as the Hokies began their journey into the ACC. They had some rough nights early in league play, including whippings handed down by Duke and North Carolina, and some surprisingly good nights. They won at Georgia Tech, and they beat N.C. State at home. When Duke came to town for the rematch,

Notes on Carlos Dixon

Name:	Carlos Ray Dixon
Born:	September 11, 1981
Hometown:	Salisbury, North Carolina
Current residence:	Salisbury, North Carolina
Occupation:	Professional basketball player with the Jiangsu Dragons in Nanjing, China, in the Chinese Basketball Association.
Position:	Forward
Height/Playing weight:	6-7, 200
Years lettered:	2001-03, 2005
Accomplishments:	Dixon was a Tech starter his entire career and averaged in double figures in scoring every year. He finished his career with 1,348 points—good for a 12.7 average. He led Tech in scoring as a sophomore, and led the Hokies in steals as a freshman and sophomore. He finished his career seventh on the career steals list with 183 and tenth in blocked shots with 90.
Nickname:	Los, Big Los
The game:	Duke at Virginia Tech, Febuary 17, 2005

Tech had a 6-6 league record and was beginning to think it had a chance at the NCAA tournament.

All it wanted against the Blue Devils was revenge. Cassell Coliseum was packed and loud as Virginia Tech took on Duke. Earlier during the season, Duke pushed around the Hokies in a 35-point victory at venerable Cameron Indoor Stadium. Afterward, Dixon promised things would be different when the teams met again at the Hokies' home.

It seemed like a bit of bluster given how convincingly Duke had dominated Tech.

"At Duke, we all just knew that we didn't get a fair shot to play Virginia Tech basketball ... we didn't play well at all, either," Dixon recalls. "For Duke to come into Cassell, we knew that they were probably going to take us a little lightly, but we knew all along that we could play with them."

Game Results

For most of the rematch, Tech was intent on proving Dixon correct. It battled the Blue Devils on even terms. Early in the second half, Duke started to pull away a little. The Blue Devils' lead grew to as many as seven points. It wasn't insurmountable, but momentum was going Duke's way.

Tech stayed within reach over the next few minutes. With a little less than nine minutes to play, the Hokies' Jeff King was fouled. King was a tight end on the football team who joined the basketball team when football ended. This was his kind of game—a rugged, physical battle—so he received more playing time than he was accustomed to.

King sunk the first foul shot. The seven-point deficit the Hokies faced earlier was down to one. But he missed the second foul attempt. The ball ended up on the floor, rolling away from the foul line to King's right, toward the Hokies' bench. His football instincts took over. King dove toward the ball and got enough of it to bat it back to teammate Jamon Gordon. Gordon whipped a pass to fellow guard Zabian Dowdell, who noticed Dixon alone in the corner. Dowdell got him the ball.

Dixon says he didn't see much between the time King missed his second foul shot and the time the ball ended up back in his hands. He and Collins were positioning themselves for a rebound when the ball squirted through the lane. By the time Dixon got to the corner, the ball was headed his way.

A broken foot turned out to be a good break for Carlos Dixon because it enabled him to play one season in the ACC.

"And I knocked down the three," Dixon says.

The shot swished through the net, and Tech, down seven less than six minutes earlier, had a two-point lead with 8:36 to play. Dixon's shot gave his teammates the confidence boost they needed.

"When he hit that shot, I knew we were going to win," Gordon says.

"That was definitely one of the deciding factors for me, too," Dixon says.

The game wasn't close to being over, though. On the other end of the court, Dixon was the primary defender on Duke's J.J. Redick, a player who would be the all-time leading scorer in the ACC by the time his career finished. On this night, Dixon did his job: Redick missed nine of his 16 shots. But one of the makes was a three-pointer with 23 seconds left, which gave Duke a one-point lead.

On the other end, Dowdell quickly answered with a three-pointer of his own to put Tech back on top. That's when Dixon and Tech did what may have been their best work of the night.

Duke ended up getting two shots in the closing seconds. Redick didn't take either one of them. Instead, Daniel Ewing took both. Keeping the ball away from Redick probably saved the Hokies' 67-65 victory.

"Carlos was just terrific on both ends during that game," Greenberg says. "The thing about Carlos in that game is that he had the poise to make the pass. He gave up of himself to make the extra pass, which is obviously so important. He did as good a job as you could do on J.J. Redick. His feel and his basketball IQ were pivotal in that game."

Dixon finished the night as Tech's high scorer with 18 points, adding nine rebounds and three assists. Plus, he earned a point in the prediction column—Tech could indeed play with Duke. The rest of the league had looked at the Hokies with a bit of wonderment as they won six of their first 12 league games. Beating Duke gives a team instant "cred" in that league. No one could say the Hokies didn't belong.

"I could not have been happier for a guy than I was for Carlos that night," says Mike Burnop, the former Tech football player who does color commentary on the football and basketball broadcasts. "He's such a good guy. ... That game was icing on the cake for him."

Greenberg doesn't disagree. He got to know Dixon well the year Dixon sat out, and knew how important it was for Dixon to finish with a big year.

Dixon promised things would be different at home for Virginia Tech against Duke, and he was right as the Hokies avenged a 35-point loss.

"That was his dream, he always wanted to play in the ACC," Greenberg says. "To see something special happen the last time around, that's a feel-good story about college athletics. That Duke game was a great example of a fifth-year guy doing whatever it took to get it done."

For Dixon, the win over Duke brought things full circle.

"That was one of the biggest games in life on any level," he says. "With me being from North Carolina and losing to Duke and North Carolina pretty badly, turning around and beating Duke was a great feeling.

"The reaction from the fans and my family and friends was great. It showed they were behind us 100 percent of the way. Along with making postseason play my last year and scoring more than 1,000 points, that game is right there at the top of my list of accomplishments."

As well it should be.

ACKNOWLEDGMENTS

I've dealt with countless sports information directors in my career. Dave Smith at Virginia Tech may be the best ever, and his help on this project reinforced that idea. Dave basically said, "What's in my office is yours," and his great staff did the same. Many thanks to Dave, Anne Panella, Donna Smith, Bryan Johnston, Bill Dyer, Torye Hurst, and photographer supreme Dave Knachel. Dave Smith also has an all-star staff of interns in Brent "Merle" Hager, Mike Cummings, and Brooke Frederickson. Every one of them did plenty to make this easier.

Football coach Frank Beamer and basketball coach Seth Greenberg are two of the easiest coaches to work with because they seem to actually like interacting with the media, and they respect what we do. Their help and the help of their staffs was invaluable. Special thanks go to Diana Clark, John Ballein, and Christie Verneil in the football office, Sharon Spradlin in the basketball office, and Russ Whitenack in the Monogram Club office.

Broadcasters Bill Roth and Mike Burnop have become friends over the years. They've helped me with many things, and this book was no different. Don't ever try to talk to them if you don't have a lot of time. Great storytellers—both of them.

Jimmy Robertson of *Hokiesports The Newspaper* is, quite simply, the man. I'm very lucky to count him as a friend and a colleague. Steve Wade is not only one of my best friends, he's an encyclopedia of Virginia Tech knowledge. His suggestions were all good, as were those of our mutual friend Chris Lang. Will Stewart, who runs a great Web site in TechSideline.Com, is another storehouse of information willing to share.

I can't forget the folks at Sports Publishing for giving me this chance. John Humenik, thanks for calling. Doug Hoepker, thanks for your incredible patience and great job editing. Whatever they're paying you, it isn't enough to have to deal with me.

My wife, Sue, and children, David and Courtney, got behind this in a big way, offering suggestions and support and never flinching when I said,

ACKNOWLEDGMENTS

"Can't do it, I have to work on the book." Love you guys, lots and lots. David takes full credit for the chapter on Ernest Wilford. His idea all the way.

Finally, thanks to the former Tech athletes who were willing to share their time and memories. This book was made possible by you.

Celebrate the Heroes of College Football
in These Other NEW Releases from Sports Publishing!

Coming in 2007!

A Tribute to Frank Beamer
by Mike Harris
• 6 x 9 hardcover
• 250 pages
• b/w photos throughout
• $24.95

The Boys from Old Florida: Inside Gator Nation
by Buddy Martin
• 6 x 9 hardcover
• 244 pages
• photos throughout
• $24.95

Don Nehlen's Tales from the West Virginia Sideline
by Don Nehlen with Shelly Poe
• 5.5 x 8.25 hardcover
• 192 pages
• photos throughout
• $19.95

Game of My Life: Alabama Crimson Tide
by Tommy Hicks
• 6 x 9 hardcover
• 256 pages
• photos throughout
• $24.95

A Chance to Win: A Complete Guide to Physical Training for Football
by Dr. Mike Gentry and Dr. Tony Caterisano
• 8.5 x 11 softcover • 300 pages
• photos throughout
• Retail: $24.95 • Now Only $14.95!

Pure Gold: Bobby Bowden: An Inside Look
by Steve Ellis and Bill Vilona
• 6 x 9 hardcover
• 192 pages
• photos throughout
• $24.95

Tiller: Not Your Average Joe
by Joe Tiller with Tom Kubat
• 6 x 9 hardcover
• 250 pages
• b/w photos throughout
• $24.95

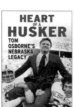

Game of My Life: LSU
by Marty Mule
• 6 x 9 hardcover
• 256 pages
• photos throughout
• $24.95

Heart of a Husker: Tom Osborne's Nebraska Legacy
by Mike Babcock
• 6 x 9 hardcover
• 256 pages
• photos throughout
• $24.95

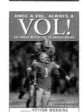

Once a Vol, Always a Vol!
by Haywood Harris and Gus Manning
• 6 x 9 hardcover
• 220 pages
• photos throughout
• $19.95

All books are available in bookstores everywhere!
Order 24-hours-a-day by calling toll-free **1-877-424-BOOK (2665)**.
Also order online at **www.SportsPublishingLLC.com**.